Toward a Healthy Marriage

Toward
a Healthy Marriage

Bernard Harnik

WORD BOOKS, PUBLISHERS
Waco, Texas

Printed in the United States of America

ISBN 0-87680-419-9

Library of Congress Catalog Card Number: 76-19541

For Ty, my good partner
in marriage
and work

Contents

Not break a bruised reed
nor quench a dimly burning wick (Isa. 42:3)
(confession of a marriage counselor)

Introduction

As I set to work on this book concerning illnesses of marriage, I received the following letter:

Dear Dr. Harnik:
I am reminded of you and your work by our twentieth wedding anniversary. At the time we consulted you, our ship of marriage had so badly listed that you had to seize the sails to turn it from the wind. However, my wife and I took the opportunity to guide the ship to its goal with new confidence. Of course, there were still many high waves that made the journey difficult, but we held fast to the rudder, as you had taught us, and again achieved clear sailing.
On the occasion of our wedding anniversary, we would like to thank you once again for your help and wish you much further success in your work.

An encouraging letter! I could be tempted toward pride were it not for other letters such as the following:

Dear Dr. Harnik:
I don't wish to appear ungrateful, for you have often helped me through dark days. But perhaps it will be useful to you if I express certain doubts in reviewing my marriage and your work as counselor. You encouraged me again and again to have patience with my husband when he needed a girlfriend. You justified your attitude by saying that a doctor—in your case, a marriage doctor—is supposed to save and preserve life rather than destroy it. Fine and good, but one must also ask what is actually being saved. I would like to illustrate what I mean by telling you an allegory.
Assume that my house is burning down. I begin to save what can still be saved. The flames make it hard for me to find what is important, let's say money and jewelry; so I grab my best flower vase and run out of the collapsing house. Afterward, I ask myself, "What use is this vase to me no matter how pretty it is and with what beautiful flowers it is filled?" This is how I feel about our marriage—burned down, only a vase in my hand.
Should you not have encouraged me to get a divorce long ago?

Every marriage counseling case is a challenge for all participants—for the counselor, for those seeking counsel, even for the immediate associates of those receiving counsel. How much experience and knowledge, love and initiative does the counselor have? How genuine is the will of those seeking counsel to overcome their difficulties? How great is their capability to recognize and solve problems? How quickly does the neighbor or relative encourage the advice-seeker to get a divorce? How well can the social environment support the counselor in his work?

In experiences with healthy and sick marriages in many countries, I have observed much that is common to and characteristic of problem marriages. I have also discovered differences in the education and culture of patients which arise from the mentality and structure of different societies. Now writing a book to American readers about the ailments of marriage, I am sustained by the experiences of many years in Europe, but I also take into consideration North American conditions.

In botany and zoology, in medicine and psychiatry, there are classifications of healthy and unhealthy specimens and people. In marriage counseling it is much more difficult to make a convincing division between healthy and unhealthy marriages. In the last chapter of my book, *Risk and Chance in Marriage,* I wrote:

> Usually very sick marriages can easily be distinguished from healthy marriages. Average marriages offer more problems, for they represent some shadowy areas between health and sickness. It is not always easy to say which is which in a marriage. It is just as difficult to answer the question of which marriage is good and which is bad. To what degree is a subjective or objective evaluation normative here? A healthy marriage in one culture or society may be a sick one in another. "Healthy" does not always mean "good," and "sick" does not always mean "bad." Ultimately the married couple must determine what they will make of their marriage and how they will experience their marriage at any given time (p. 176).

Nevertheless I mentioned in this connection some typical characteristics of marital disturbance—fear, aggressiveness, a feeling of not being understood, jealousy, and mistrust. And I closed:

> The advantage of knowing whether or not a marriage is healthy or sick is quite obvious. A sick marriage should be brought to a specialist for treatment as soon as possible; the feeling that "we have a good marriage" will heighten the sense of happiness in that marriage (p. 177).

One can attempt to classify disturbed or sick marriages, but of what value is such information for those seeking counsel? Obviously, a sick person should seek a doctor and not try to treat himself. What sick person can be healed by reading a treatise concerning his illness? Just as all comparisons are to some degree imprecise, so is the comparison of illness in the medical sense and marital illness. One who reads books about such matters can often recognize the nature of the problems that trouble his or her marriage and can perhaps even find the solution without the aid of a professional therapist. At least he or she can become aware that expert treatment is necessary. A person with a sick marriage who is well read can also better judge and support the counseling efforts of an expert.

PART I

Mrs. Nora Miller: A Case History

1: What Kind of Therapy?

The task of classifying marriage illnesses is complicated by great differences among psychological and counseling schools of thought. When a Freudian uses the term *libido,* he has a completely different concept in mind than does a Jungian. Further, if a Freudian employs the expression *father complex,* one assumes that it is to be associated with the concept of the Oedipus complex. However, a Jungian would perhaps refer to the *archetypical father.*

And what is one to say of the different methods? Should one deal with persons seeking counsel in a direct or indirect manner? Should one engage in dialogue or simply allow counselees to talk? Give advice? Allow persons to learn by themselves what they need? Speak to them about faith, pray with them?

In the early days of psychotherapy, counseling almost always took the form of classical psychoanalysis—couch, indirective, frequent sessions lasting many months or years. One had to keep dogmatically to the teachings of Freud in order not to be suspected of charlatanism. Today any method is received in good faith if it is successful. This is especially true for marriage counseling which involves not only the individual but two partners, their relationship, and the marriage as a special community with specific standards. If one extends counseling to family counseling, or family therapy, then the situation really is much more complicated than that which leads a person suffering from fear neurosis to the psychotherapist.

It is not my purpose here to discuss the advantages or disadvantages of this or that school or method of marriage counseling. I will, however, present my position and describe how I do it. The simplest thing would be to say that I am "eclectic," but since that expression is so imprecise, perhaps the following explanation will clarify what I intend by it.

In my practice, the patient who is having trouble in his or her marriage or with his or her family is evaluated in two ways: functionally and uniquely. The following drawing illustrates the components that evidence themselves in these two ways:

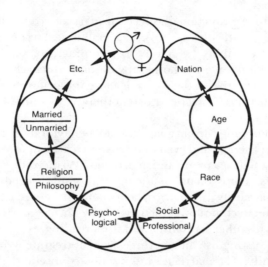

The whole person presents himself or herself as the functional aspects, façades, or identities shown by the circles. The identification of a person with his or her functions is called *persona* or *masque,* and the unknown, the X, is symbolized by *heart, name, faith, agape, mystery,* xpictos (equals Christ).

This double view allows access not only to functional problems—

extroversion, introversion, neurotic behavior, inhibition, depression, fears of the individual, and so on—but also to the "person" lying behind the façades.

The same holds true for the entirety of any marriage or any family. One must deal with the functional aspects—living, sexual union, problems of contrasts, and so on—and also with the mysterious, archetypical, religious, mystical aspects.

The counselor's attitude toward the patient and toward the marriage (family) is accordingly objective, neutral, technical, psychological, sociological, and juridical and at the same time respectful, subjective, amazed, sympathetic, personal. This description originates with Dr. Paul Tournier, founder of the so-called medicine of the whole person with which I have been closely associated for more than two decades.

In regard to the functional aspects in marriage counseling, I proceed as undogmatically as possible, sometimes recommending a classical psychoanalysis (which I do not practice). Occasionally I advise a more intensive psychotherapy of some other school in which case the representative of the school is more important to me than its doctrine. Sometimes I practice a psychotherapy in which I use dream analysis.

My methods range from analytical to behavioral therapy to accompaniment therapy and even to intensive treatment for the support of weak personalities or invalid marriages. With young or middle-aged patients, I use Freudian ideas. With middle-aged and older patients I use mostly Jungian concepts, and in between I utilize all kinds of other techniques gained from my own experiences, from association with other specialists, and from reading.

Basically I distinguish among three types of treatment for marriage and the family: (1) marriage and family counseling; (2) psychotherapeutic marriage and family counseling (marriage and family therapy); and (3) pastoral marriage and family counseling.

Marriage and family counseling represents the sum of the advice, recommendations, suggestions, communication of knowledge and facts, and help of all sorts which the counselor gives to the patient and whereby the counselor essentially appeals to the patient's reason. The goal of such counseling is to help the one seeking counsel out of an acute or chronic marital or family difficulty. This work can take a few weeks or a period of years, depending on the nature of the problem. It is carried out by a more or less schooled and qualified counselor. It deals with the majority of marriage difficulties and can be compared to the work of the general practitioner of medicine. It is different from but not less important than psychotherapeutic marriage and family counseling.

Psychotherapeutic marriage and family counseling is used for the most part in cases of mentally disturbed (neurotic, psychopathological, depressive, and so on) marriages and families. It requires the services of a person who has had many years of specialized psychotherapeutic or psychiatric training, who has generally been associated with an apprenticeship in analysis, and who has a great deal of experience. The goal of this type therapy, like marriage and family counseling, is to free the patient from his or her marital problems. But in addition the therapist seeks to further the individual's process of maturing, sometimes without reference to the fate of the marriage. This is a field for specialists whose number falls far short of the needs of the populace. Because of the counselor's education and because of the amount of time involved with this sort of treatment, psychotherapeutic marriage counseling is expensive.

Pastoral counseling in marital and family problems requires the services of a person with theological and psychological education. Its essential goal is to surmount the patient's difficulties with specific religious elements. Prayer and intercession may be used; the counselor may attempt to awaken insights by exchanging ideas and listening, by expressing love toward the patient and toward his or her fellow man, and by integrating the patient into a Christian congregation. Along with the immediate purpose of marriage and family counseling, the pastor strives to open or broaden the patient's horizon into the religious world. He discusses the question of guilt, not only from the psychological point of view, but in light of the Bible. He can also speak of grace and forgiveness. In the Christian sense, this confessional exchange differs from a patient's frank articulation of feelings and thoughts to a psychotherapist.

Each of the three types of counseling has its special characteristics, but since all strive for a common goal—to help the patient—the boundaries between them are fluid. It might well be that a "common, everyday" counselor can achieve impressive psychotherapeutical results if through his counseling a patient matures or develops insights. A psychotherapist often helps a patient achieve a more mature relationship to God when he is able to open up choked feelings. And of course a pastor can succeed by Christian brotherly love in leading a patient out of isolation into a new relationship with his or her mate or family members.

In addition to length of study and type of counseling, there is the matter of the counselor himself. A mature counselor is, in general, more successful in marriage counseling than an immature psychotherapist in spite of the better education of the latter. A hypocritical pastor is more than problematical in marriage counseling, no matter how many good schools he has attended. A humane or personally oriented psychotherapist can be effective in a pastoral way even if he knows nothing of the Bible. If a person is seeking a counselor, he or she should have a full understanding of the different types of therapists as well as the type of problem and the personality of the therapist.

2: Background of the Case

In order to demonstrate the various types of counseling and therapeutic procedures I make use of in my practice, and in order to show how the techniques flow into and out of one another, I want to share the experiences of one of my patients, Mrs. Nora Miller. From time to time I will interject counseling or psychological comments, but for the most part, Nora will tell her own story.

Especially in the beginning I had to be satisfied with general counseling methods. In a second stage, analytical discussions of dreams combined with careful reflection. Religious counseling was also employed.

Mr. and Mrs. Miller came for counseling because they no longer knew what to do about their eleven-year-old Ann. The little girl, who up to that time had been a good pupil in the fifth grade, suddenly no longer wanted to go to school. She gave no reason for her refusal but was obviously afraid. Of what? The parents could not explain. The teacher was not a sympathetic person, but Ann's extraordinary behavior could not be blamed on the teacher. Ann's relationships to her thirteen-year-old .sister and her ten-year-old brother were apparently normal. The worst thing was that she refused to speak or cooperate with a child psychologist. Every time she was brought to the psychologist, there was a scene, and the parents had lost hope for a reasonable solution.

Someone recommended that the parents bring Ann to me. I had no more success than my colleagues; so I invited the entire family for a counseling session. Viewed diagnostically, this meeting indicated a pathological family structure. Mrs. Miller did not try to hide the fact that she considered her husband, William, stupid and that she did not take him seriously. As could be expected, the oldest girl, identifying with her father, took sides against her mother. Obviously, the boy was the mother's favorite. And in the middle Ann, a typical "sandwich child," toilsomely struggled for her identity. She was sensitive and nervous like Mrs. Miller, but she took a position between her mother and father.

Family therapy, or at least marriage therapy, based upon psychotherapeutic principles and lasting at least one to two years was needed, but the parents did not want to wait that long for Ann to go back to school. We decided upon a drastic cure: Ann was sent to a boarding school in the Alps where she had to bite the bullet and accept reality. She was at the top of her class academically, but personally she was refractory. Finally she succeeded, after a three-month stay, in being accepted at home again. She returned to her former school as if nothing had happened.

But now let us allow Nora to speak:

I could see that our marriage had to be healed, but how? At first I thought William absolutely had to go to the psychiatrist because he always made such childish jokes. I could not take him seriously. Nevertheless, he was successful in his work. Then, as Dr. Harnik put it, I took my projection away from him and declared that I was ready to go into treatment, especially since William refused to do so. He nevertheless supported my decision.

I knew only too well how much I needed intensive therapy. My childhood had been a nightmare. Years ago I had been in psychotherapy with a pastor. In addition, I was disturbed by my failure in sexual relations with my husband. At best, I merely gave him satisfaction. I would have preferred no sexual relations at all. The reverse side of William's infantile manner was his unflagging loyalty. It would never have occurred to him to keep another woman or to reproach me. He was understanding about my sexual frigidity. Besides these marital difficulties, I felt I lacked normal feelings in other significant relationships. I hated my mother whom I visited from time to time.

In counseling work two points require attention at the very beginning: (1) Are there observable relationships between earlier experiences and an actual problem whereby a diagnostic but not therapeutic insight can be gained? (2) The first so-called affective contact between the counselor and the patient determines whether or not treatment can be attempted. If the contact is bad, if something doesn't click between the two participants, treatment should generally be terminated before it really begins. If the contact is good, there is hope although successful treatment is by no means assured.

Sigmund Freud was the first to note that the relationship between patient and therapist is essentially built upon projections and is therefore subject to change. At best there will be, after some months of therapy, a positive transferral of early childhood feelings to the psychotherapist as father or mother image. In working with these feelings the real process of healing begins as the patient becomes conscious of suppressed traumatic feelings, experiences, conflicts, or wishes.

At first I had some difficulty with Nora. She seemed so lacking in feeling that in her presence I felt as if I were in a deep freeze. I knew her feelings were there, but they were suppressed, dammed up, blockaded. The effect of her personality on me elicited anything but sympathy. However, Nora was physically attractive. In order to overcome this zero point in our beginning relationship, I took flight into fantasy. I looked through her—as it seemed to me—cold façade into her real being, her X, her Christ within. Only after our relationship developed and her suppression of feeling decreased was I able to feel comfortable in her presence without recourse to this artifice of the imagination. In regard to the development of her feelings and wishes for contact with me, let her speak:

With mixed feelings I anticipated the first meeting with the person who was to steer our lost ship of marriage and family in the right direction again. So much was at stake. Thank God, I was able to react positively to him. It is not easy to tell one's problems to a complete stranger, much less to talk about one's failures. In our first meeting I spoke with halting voice and tears in my eyes, wishing my husband would assume this task for me. But William contented himself with simply making a few remarks at the end of my presentation. In doing so he made a face which expressed the pain he felt about the misfortune he had endured.

In a second meeting, this time alone, I had to tell about my life. It was so painful. After a few more sessions, Dr. Harnik received both my husband and me. A hateful scene developed between us, and we made mutual accusations. Actually I was glad this happened because we had playacted long enough. Now everything that had been poisoning our relationship was coming out. Dr. Harnik limited himself to making some suggestions for standards of behavior and left up to us whether or not we would come back.

Meanwhile, summer vacation came, and I was concerned as to whether Dr. Harnik was even willing to continue the treatment. Perhaps he had reasons against it. For instance, age—I was forty-six and William forty-seven—or the hopelessness of the case after the negative experiences I had had years before. I went through some anxious weeks because I didn't know what I would do without help. I could have spared myself these worries, for after the vacation Dr. Harnik again took up the treatment. At first I was relieved, not because I had given myself over to the illusion that he would finally solve my problems, but because I was thoroughly convinced that he would find out what was really wrong. I hoped he would be stronger than I, that is, stronger than all the negative things in me, and that with his help I would be able to emerge from my great confusion.

At this point, it might be well to refer to that type of projection which relates to the archetype of the healer. The term *archetype,* which Carl Jung made one of the pillars of his doctrinal structure, is a psychological expression arising from generations of experience extending over thousands of years. It is a form of prototype residing in our so-called collective subconscious—as distinguished from our personal subconscious—which in certain circumstances can be awakened.

In Nora's case, hope for recovery emerged from her innermost being as a conviction that I could cure her. She had projected upon me her archetype of the healer. Other such universal human images—as distinguished from personal human images—are father or mother, the Great Mother, the priest, the tribal chieftain, love, death, resurrection, Savior, Christ, God, and so on. In marriage counseling such a projection can be useful, but since a withdrawal of the projections eventually occurs, leading to a sense of disappointment, such a treatment can only remain useful if in its course a valuable personal relationship has been established.

It was decided that I was to come for counseling because I was the only one who felt under pressure and the only one who saw the necessity of a change in our marital and family relationships. At the beginning of this new phase of treatment I related particulars out of my past. When I told Dr. Harnik about an earlier psychotherapy, I mentioned that the therapist, a pastor, said I had Lesbian tendencies. I could not even say the word *Lesbian*. I felt too ashamed. Not only that, but I didn't know exactly what it meant. Dr. Harnik apparently noticed my embarrassment and anxiety, for he said, "Well, that can be cured too." Only six words, but they were like a healing ointment on my soul and became an island of refuge when the waves of depression threatened to sweep over me. For every encouraging word, no matter how seldom, I was grateful and took it into my everyday life. Everything in me was desolate, empty, cold, but with Dr. Harnik I found warmth, security, fatherly feelings, everything I urgently sought. I was embarrassed to seem so starved, and I had to remember not to beg for his affection, for that seemed disgraceful.

One afternoon in the summer I met our children at the swimming pool after I had been to see Dr. Harnik. I was filled with feelings of happiness over having found a father. Then I discovered at the swimming pool that I in fact did have Lesbian tendencies. Perhaps I allowed them to surface because I believed Dr. Harnik when he said they could be removed under certain circumstances. In the following weeks such feelings and thoughts recurred. Sometimes strong, sometimes faint, they wavered between my subconscious and my conscious. Often they frightened me.

On the one hand, I was happy to be able to go to Dr. Harnik. On the other, from time to time I had to fight resistance which arose when I thought about a coming visit. One night I awakened in fear with the thought, "Tomorrow you must go to Dr. Harnik!" When I was sitting in the car waiting to go into his office, I was again seized by fear and wished I could hold fast to something, but I didn't know what. Even today I have similar feelings. In the early sessions when I sat across from Dr. Harnik, I became petrified, as with my husband, but that situation improved. Still I have not succeeded in reacting in a relaxed manner and in being outgoing. Often I wept after a counseling session because of this.

During a period of my treatment, the chief work was in the discussion of dreams. Often I was embarrassed to discover how much bad emerged from my sunconscious. If a person could die of shame, I would have been dead long ago. Once when I sought not to see the real interpretation, Dr. Harnik held up before my eyes my low, disgusting inclinations. He was certainly right in doing this, for I had to be honest with myself. But at the time I felt his statements were exaggerated, and they hurt me.

Because of schedule difficulties, he made my next appointment for fourteen days later. I considered this punishment. I lived as if in fear of death and wept often. Lacking any self-confidence and trust, I interpreted everything to my disadvantage. If the space of time between appointments was longer than a week, I began to believe that Dr. Harnik didn't care about me. Once when he scheduled me for several appointments close together, my joy knew no bounds. Immediately I felt secure.

After a couple of months I became aware of how slowly I was progressing, and I panicked. I believed that Dr. Harnik would lose his patience and give up on me, just as the pastor had done. I gathered all my courage and told Dr. Harnik I was afraid of losing him. I was infinitely relieved when he answered he would stay with me and help me until I was able to make it on my own. I thank God daily that he led me to this man.

When I again related in self-criticism that I could not offer my husband what he needed sexually, Dr. Harnik said that it was possible to get along without sex. I was shocked at the thought. No, it could not work. My husband had often declared that he could not give up our sex life, and I needed William's love, his support, his tenderness. If I were to withdraw from him sexually, I would have to face the possibility of losing his love. It would indeed be dreadful to accept his tenderness and then withdraw from him when he began to approach the high point and natural conclusion of intimacy. Naturally I was also afraid that he would seek from another woman what he did not get from me.

Dr. Harnik did not return to this point again. Apparently he was only asking a test question. Occasionally the fear arose in me that I would never again become psychologically healthy. Then I was seized by overwhelming desolation, hate, rage, and repugnance toward all the compulsions to which I am subject, as well as aversion toward life in general. Often I feel I have never really been loved.

In the course of treatment, my Lesbian feelings and desires came more and more strongly into my consciousness. Occasionally they occurred with a force I never would have expected. I recognized that they originated with my mother, and it became clear why I had always both feared and longed for her, hated and needed her. Even today our relationship is troubled. Dr. Harnik said I should at first simply accept these feelings. This was hard. I was afraid they would remain and prove a catastrophe for my marriage or stand between me and my husband. Meanwhile, I began to notice small signs of progress. Then the idea emerged that I could easily give up my Lesbian tendencies if I could exchange them for something better.

Gradually my attitude toward Dr. Harnik changed. At first I simply stretched out my empty hands toward him and waited for his help. I saw in him a substitute mother, and figuratively speaking, like a small child I clung to him. And this at the age of forty-seven! If it were not a matter for weeping, I would have to laugh. Sometimes I wonder why my husband did not help me along.

Summer vacation is almost here again. Dark shadows lurk in the background, and they will overtake me as soon as I leave Dr. Harnik. But I believe and firmly hope that the evil powers which torment me will someday be conquered.

After the vacation I got the impression that Nora was a bit freer. At any rate she was able to enjoy the time with her family. I was reminded of a colleague who periodically left his practice for a few weeks. He maintained that his patients were always better after his absence. He understood this as a specific therapy and called it "absento therapy."

3: Using Dream Analysis

Before I go into the meaning of Nora's life history for the purpose of understanding her conflicts and problems, I would like to discuss my attitude toward dream therapy. Nora mentioned in her account that we discussed dreams. In her case this actually represented the greatest part of our work. In less than a year she remembered, wrote down, and interpreted about four hundred dreams of varying lengths. Sigmund Freud considered the psychological ramifications of the dream so important that he called it the Via Regia to the subconscious. Physiological studies have shown that people dream several times during one night's sleep and that the psychological equilibrium is disturbed when dreams are interrupted.

Essentially Freud saw in the dream the magical or symbolical expression of subconscious memories, feelings, or "thoughts." According to Freud, dreams are primarily wish-fulfillment. Often the wish-fulfillment is so hidden that it is not recognizable, especially when the so-called superego, a type of social conscience, morally rejects the wish. The resistance of the subconscious to attempts to uncover the hidden wish can become so strong that the patient quite simply ceases to remember dreams. If the work with the dream is successful, its symbolic content is interpreted, and the deeper, suppressed, and forgotten content of the subconscious is penetrated. The disclosure or elucidation of subconscious psychological "complexes" leads to their objectivization and to a release of the patient's tensions. This is one basis for the cure of neurotic patients. The other consists in manipulating transferral problems.

Even to Alfred Adler the dream meant wish-fulfillment. According to him, the subconscious is less filled with sexual fantasies than with ideas of self-assertion and power. Because the child in his weakness develops an inferiority complex, the subconscious reacts with compensatory dreams. So, in dreams one can achieve the victory denied in everyday life.

For Carl Jung the dream had not only and not always and perhaps not at all a biographical content, but it primarily represented images from the collective subconscious. He believed the experiences of all mankind were reflected in dreams and thus they had an archetypical character. However, Jung felt the dream had a mostly compensatory function in that it gave a solution to the limitations of conscious life. Thus an extrovert dreams of introversion, the logical thinker dreams on an emotional level, and so on. During an intensive individuation phase—a process of maturing when there is a harmonization of opposites and the development of the so-called self—dreams produce images of wholeness (mandala forms and the cross) and images of birth (snakes and a small child). Often dreams have a prospective or prophetic character.

Freud, as well as Jung, pointed out that the symbolic language of dreams parallels the symbolism of folk legends and fairy tales. The well-known motif of the Oedipus legend is mirrored, according to Freud, in the so-called Oedipus complex of the man who as a boy looked upon his father as a rival for his mother, just as Oedipus killed his father and married his mother. The corresponding female complex—the Electra complex—finds its parallel in the story of Electra who incited her brother Orestes to kill her mother to avenge the mother's deception of the father.

Jung also relied upon mythology to discover the archetypical character of his patients' dreams. Dreams of individuation have images similar to those found in many religions where there is the figure of a savior or redeemer in the form of a small child. Bunyan's *Pilgrim's Progress* expresses spiritual maturation. The Book of Job deals with the suffering servant, and each of us carries in his subconscious the great half-indignant question directed to God. "Why?" Universal humanity is repeatedly reflected in the subconscious of the individual.

Existential analysts always interpret the dreams of their patients in relation to the present. Many psychotherapists make no use whatsoever of dream interpretation.

It is a rule of thumb that individuals must interpret their dreams themselves and that, at most, the analyst should merely guide them in understanding the symbols. This may explain the fact that most patients produce dreams which correspond to the expectations of their analysts. One could then ask, What objective value can dream interpretation have? None at all. Dreams have only a subjective value. What is important is what the patient recognizes or feels, not what could be derived from an objective view of the dream.

I am convinced that it is not the correct or incorrect interpretation of dreams which has a curative effect but the relationship of the patient to the psychotherapist. One could regularly play chess with the patient and come to just as rapid and good results as through work with dreams. That may sound heretical, but children's game-therapy which proceeds without interpretation supports my conviction.

Nevertheless I practice dream-interpretation in my psychotherapeutically based marriage consultation. In many cases I use it in counseling sessions with married couples or members of a family in order to activate a more intimate relationship. But in interpretation I do not hold to the theory of any particular school. Whenever, for example, religious images emerge, I may make Jungian interpretations in the sense of the process of individuation, but I try also to take into consideration the purely religious needs of the client.

Perhaps that is the result of personal experience. As a very young doctor, I had a serious infection which produced intense fever fantasies with religious content. I understood them according to Freud as a religious superstructure of uncontrolled sexual wishes. Later, after I became familiar with the psychology of Jung, I inclined to see them as compensating for my atheistic philosophy of the time. In reality—so I am convinced—they were actually God calling me through my subconscious to return to him. My conscious resistance then was strong. Four years later at the age of twenty-eight my reason "capitulated," and I dedicated myself to the invisible Christ.

How unorthodox dream interpretation has become in general is shown in the example of an Italian colleague of mine who does not hesitate to occasionally discuss her own dreams with her clients. If Freud could hear that, he would turn over in his grave!

From the multitude of dreams which I discussed with Nora, I will quote only a few with her description and interpretation.

> I lay in a hospital shortly before an eye operation. I was afraid. A few feet away lay a man whom I had known earlier. "Will you love me?" I asked him. I thought that would at least be a comfort. When he made a face as if he did not want to obligate himself, I said, "Only until the operation is over." Then he laughed, embraced me, and went away.
>
> My mother came and said, "You mustn't be afraid. It won't hurt. It's nothing at all."
>
> "Go away!" I cried. "Mama, you know very well that isn't true. And the injections into the eye and the bandaging?"
>
> "Yes, that too," she affirmed. But I felt she only wanted to make herself seem important.
>
> I was still having my period. I hoped no one saw. I tried to pull up the blanket and the sheet that lay jumbled at the foot of the bed. Something was wrong with the bedspread too. Then I heard the doctor outside and was afraid. "Now he will come in at any moment." The thing I dreaded most was being bandaged. I was so afraid that I wouldn't be able to bear it and that I would no longer be able to defend myself or to leave. I was terrified.
>
> The doctor and his aide came in. They stood at the door and conversed excitedly. I looked at him. He resembled a pediatrician who had once treated our children. He looked like someone who could be trusted. That was something which until now I had not taken into account, the human relationship. If only my trust were stronger than my fear! When he stepped to my bed, I thought I would have to tell him the truth, and so I told him I suffered from a neurosis and had a great fear of fits. "Yes," he said, "haven't you consulted your doctor about this operation? Don't you know how many have died from attacks of coughing, fits, and other things?"
>
> "No," I answered. He applied ointment to my wrist. What that had to do with an eye operation I don't know. On my left wrist was a blue band.
>
> "Are you with the United Nations?" he asked.
>
> "I was with the United Nations," I answered.
>
> "In what capacity?"

I thought feverishly but simply could not remember. I only knew that it had something to do with school management.

"Then you had too much free time?" he asked.

"No, that's just it. That's why I left," was my answer. By now he had the hypodermic needle in his hand, and the situation had become threatening. "What shall I do now?" I asked. "Phone the doctor?" It was already about ten o'clock, and I thought Dr. Harnik would be at home.

"Be calm and sit down in an armchair for awhile, and consider, and then ask one of the children," he said.

Indeed a couple of children were jumping around in the room. "But I can't ask children in such an important matter," I thought.

Nora's interpretation supplemented by my comments yielded the following thoughts:

I am in need of treatment, and so my sight-insight was to be restored. Did this concern my masculine nature, my animus? Or did it deal with a potential sexual partner? My question as to whether he loved me could refer to both. His refusal to become involved represents my difficulties in forming relationships and my inner resistance to my husband. In the dream I console myself with the reference "until the operation is over."

In the next image my mother appears. Does she represent a benign Magna Mater who wants to relieve me of my anxiety? Or is it an image of my real mother who is functioning as a form of conscience? The dialogue with her indicates my relationship to her. In any case I reject her even at the subconscious level. The relationship with her and with sexual fantasies are elucidated in the image of the menstrual period and the reaction of shame associated with it. Naturally it could also indicate a resistance to growing up. The appearance of the physician at first awakens in me a fear of being bandaged. This fear dominates my subconscious. The physician within me asserts itself and brings me help.

The memory of the pediatrician refers to difficulties in my childhood. I knew of course that Dr. Harnik had also been a pediatrician! My subconscious hope is supported by a compassionate relationship with him. In the dream I recognize my anxiety neurosis.

Interestingly enough, it is reported from ancient times that patients who came for a cure at a place of healing—for instance, Epidauros in Greece, where there was a temple in honor of Asklepios, the god of healing—could see the healing god in the so-called temple sleep wherein he revealed to them the diagnosis of their illness. On the next day they brought the revealed diagnosis to the priest who then prescribed a suitable remedy. This anticipates the procedure of modern psychotherapy. The patient receives insight from his own subconscious—his revelation—and discusses the "diagnosis" with his physician-priest.

The inner dialogue between Nora and the operating doctor concerns dying. As a rule this dream symbol has a thoroughly positive character because it indicates the demise of earlier images stemming from childhood.

The application of ointment to the wrist is reminiscent of the anointment of priests and kings and thus expresses a process of maturing, of becoming healthy. The wrists are to be made more mobile. I am to emerge from my stiffness. My hands, the expression of my personality, are to become more capable of function. The United Nations symbolizes peace and indicates the conquest of my psychological conflicts. The association with school (school management) reminds me of many conflicts about school problems. Perhaps it also indicates a process of learning or maturing.

In reality I have little time. The dream may be a warning to take more time for reflection, perhaps also for prayer. The needle in the hand of the physician might be a phallic symbol which threatens me sexually. It is also an implement of healing which I at first resist. Telephoning the doctor means communicating with the archetype of the healer. With "ten o'clock" (es ist zehn uhr) I associate the Swiss-German phrase "s'isch zähni" (in English, something like gorgeous) and refer it to Dr. Harnik and a complete readiness to be helped. In fact, the advice to be calm and to consult the children who are present comes from him. Thereby I am reminded of Christ's words that one must become as a little child to enter the kingdom of heaven. My reasonable self is amazed in the dream that such an important matter as my process of maturing is to be solved by a child. Perhaps by the conquest of my infantile attitude? By understanding my childhood?

Nora seemed particularly impressed by this dream. In Jungian psychology, dreams with archetypical images which make a great

impression upon the dreamer are given the honorary title Great
Dreams.

It was morning. I found myself in my parents' bedroom. I was supposed to tidy up the beds and the room. My mother had gone away
for a few days, and I was to take her place. I decided not to clean
the room thoroughly. Mother could do that herself since she was
supposed to be back in the evening.

The room was in great disorder, and I couldn't decide where to
begin. When I took the covers off the bed, I noticed they were those
of my own bedroom. I picked up my father's pajamas and suddenly
saw they were my husband's. The collar was soiled, and I pondered
whether I should take the pajamas with me to wash. I stood there
undecided, looked at the collar, and saw that it really was very dirty.
I decided to take the pajamas with me for washing and thought how
mother would see father that evening in clean pajamas. At the same
time, I thought that these clean pajamas were my husband's.

Then in the dream I awakened from a noon nap approximately at
the same time my husband awakened. William wanted sex, but I
indicated I was not particularly enthusiastic about it. He tried to
persuade me. The moment he came to my bed, the doorbell rang. I
listened and wondered who it might be. I heard someone go down
the steps and assumed it was a man who might think no one was at
home. I had left the window of my parents' bedroom open and
looked through it onto the street. Then I awakened.

In interpreting this dream I am immediately aware of my childhood and my sexual resistance. The dream begins in the morning in
my parents' bedroom. Even as a child my fantasies were taken up
with the secrets of grownups behind bedroom doors. Straightening
up the room relates to my present psychotherapeutic work: I am
tidying up my uncontrolled childhood.

Obviously my subconscious is aware of great disorder in relationship to sexual fantasies. I transfer my ideas concerning father and
mother to my husband and myself. Perhaps Freud was right in saying that little girls want their fathers as sexual partners. Consciously
I would violently reject this idea. I associate sexual things with
something dirty, as is emphasized by the collar I am concerned
about others seeing. My intention of washing the pajamas indicates
my subconscious desire to clean up my fantasy. At the conclusion
of this dream sequence, the identification between my father and
my husband is again expressed. Also in the second part of the dream

this relationship becomes clear. Resistance to my husband's desires may originate in the fact that I see in him my father whose sexual approach would have to awaken feelings of guilt and resistance in me. The resistance is then strengthened by the belief that someone —the man downstairs at the door and in the street below my parents' bedroom, that is, in the subconscious—could see us. My sexual taboo is obviously supported by the superego too.

From Freud come three doctrines: (1) infantile sexuality; (2) manipulating drives such as sublimation, suppression, conversion, and perversion; and (3) the three stages—the ego, the id (instinctual drive), and the superego (an extended conscience formed by parental and social ideas regarding morality).

The next dream also had something to do with washing, however, the strangeness of the place makes me think of an archetypical interpretation. The previous dream occurred in a completely different phase of my work and was obviously on a biographical level.

In this dream I was standing with my mother in an unfamiliar kitchen in front of a large washing machine. I was explaining to her how the machine worked. We were going to wash a towel. I opened the machine and stuffed the towel into a pipe in the upper part, but I was not at all sure whether I had put it in the right place. I rather believed that the opening for loading was down lower. Next to the pipe was a section containing the motor. I started the machine and thought, "I will now actually see whether it runs properly or whether I have done something wrong."

A corner of the towel, a dust cloth, was protruding. Now a flame appeared in the motor, and I was convinced that a fire would break out. Immediately I stopped the machine, but it had already begun to burn. My mother stood behind me leaning against a table. I hurried past her, looking feverishly for a container of water large enough to put it out. Instead of helping, my mother put her hands to her face and screamed. I found a bucket and threw water on the fire. I believe I succeeded in putting it out.

The interpretation of this dream can be made completely on a psychoanalytical basis using Freudian theories. The washing machine was to cleanse the "dirty" fantasies of the dreamer—the conflict with the mother, the phallic symbol of the pipe, the fire of sexual drive.

Suppressing the flame was putting out the fire of unacceptable desire. But Nora interpreted the dream with images she had taken from Jungian psychology. It is possible there was a mechanism underlying them which is called "flight into spirituality," a phenomenon often met in outspokenly fanatical representatives of religion or philosophy who consider sexuality taboo. Freud was the first to refer to this, but at the same time he, in my opinion, overshot his target when he called religion an illusion and assessed it to be totally unreal.

The unfamiliar kitchen and the large washing machine make me think of an important maturing phase in my individuation. My mother is probably the personified Magna Mater.

This archetype recalls the tribal mothers, priestesses, and prophetesses of many peoples, who were gifted with special spiritual powers and had great authority. They were reverently loved, often feared, and finally hated when they dominated and suppressed the legitimate needs of the individual. Then they received the aspects of the domineering mother who hinders the maturing process of her children.

My explanation as to how the machine functioned shows that my subconscious had knowledge of certain inner relationships. The towel symbolizes the fabric of my soul, my subconscious, my life. The upper part of the machine represents the conscious, the intellectual, and I feel I am trying to solve the problem at the wrong place. My dream-consciousness knows better. It seeks the opening for loading further down, in a deeper level, in the subconscious, perhaps in the collective subconscious. The motor reveals my motivations, and I am made conscious that they could run in a perverse direction. In fact, a corner of my existence is dusty, that is, old-fashioned, superfluous, antiquated, disturbing. No wonder it begins to burn. It is only right that everything superfluous is destroyed, burned up. At first the Magna Mater stands there calmly since I am occupied with putting out the fire. But this is precisely what I am not supposed to do because the fire is needed to destroy the old and to allow the new to arise—like the phoenix. For this reason the Magna Mater within me cries out.

I wanted to buy a summer dress and had in mind a certain color of green. In the bus on the way to the city, I suddenly thought,

"Why have I settled on this color? The dress could just as well be red or some other color." At the dress shop I asked for a summer dress. The salesgirl explained that she had none, that people didn't wear summer dresses any more. I was rather astonished. "What in the world does one wear in the summer if not a summer dress?"

Then suddenly I found myself in the forest with my girlfriend from school. We were sitting at the edge of a road arguing about the summer dress. She said, "You don't need a new dress. At home I always wear my old clothes."

"Even if I don't need one," I answered, "I will buy a new one anyway, and you should get something new yourself."

During this discussion people were constantly walking past us. I saw, on the other side of the road coming out of the forest, the former mayor of our town who is now studying theology. I watched him cross the street and disappear into the forest, but I thought, "I had better stop looking or he will be noticed."

This dream probably expressed a phase of individuation, for it concerned something new. Perhaps it even indicated a deepening of my religious life. It may be related to the passage from Revelation, "See, I make all things new," or to new clothes for the feast in the kingdom of God. The summer dress relates to summer, that is, the middle of life where I now am, a high point in the process of maturing in the Jungian doctrine of individuation. Green equals hope, fullness of life. The bus represents my nonpersonal psychical aspects. In arguing with them, the attempt emerges to remain young and to prefer red, the color of passion. The salesgirl, another inner part of me with whom I enter into dialogue, reminds me of growing old.

All characters in a dream represent one's own interests and are to be regarded subjectively rather than objectively. One must always ask what characteristics of the dreamer they express. A salesgirl offers what one needs but also what one rejects.

On a deeper level of my subconscious—in the forest—I discover an aid to maturing—the girlfriend from school, a helper in the learning process—for a lively dialogue takes place. This is probably the instrument by which antithetical contrasts are expressed. In this there is the difficulty of replacing the old with the new. How hard it is in real life to part with old junk! No wonder this is even more difficult in the psychical area.

I am confronted with anonymous surroundings, but an animus figure appears, the mayor. He has a religious aspect, for he is studying theology. This masculine image, which I probably suppress, comes into the picture from a deeper level, from the forest. That he again moves toward the right, toward the masculine side, probably corresponds to his function. Instead of accepting him in my structure, I suppress him because I am afraid of the moral judgment of society.

I was sitting in a restaurant, waiting for my husband. Outside at some distance an auto race was taking place. I saw many spectators and heard the loud clattering and howling of the engines. After a while, the race was over, and the restaurant slowly filled with people. I also saw some friends from school coming in. I wondered why my husband was taking so long.

Through the window I suddenly saw Mary, our oldest daughter. She turned the corner of a building and came across the now-empty street to the restaurant. She was much younger than she is now and made a pitiful impression. She slumped over and walked with her arms dangling down. Her head hung to the left, and she appeared to have been crying. The worst part was her gait. She didn't really walk but dragged her feet along the ground. She wore no socks or shoes, only wooden clogs. Suddenly she stubbed her left foot and stumbled, but I could not see it clearly. She almost fell down, and she began to weep. I stood up and hurried over to her. I took her by the arm and said something to her, but after awakening I could not remember what it was.

In my attempt to interpret this dream I was at first struck by the disturbed relationship with my husband: his tireless attitude of expectation in regard to sex, my constant fear of it, my sexual coldness, his unmasculine attitude, my constant disappointment about it, our differences in raising the children, the impudence of my oldest girl, my jealousy toward her when she takes my husband's part against me. Did I want—in the dream—to make her younger? To degrade her? To stand in the way of her life as my mother had done with me? But when I proceeded systematically, still other motifs came to mind. The restaurant could be a place of sexual fulfillment but also of spiritual nourishment. The man upon whom I waited did not necessarily have to be my husband but simply *the* man, the masculine, the animus. This fits in with the masculine world outside (the auto race), the many people, the loud clattering and howling of the engines.

Finally, my inner being has occasionally resembled the noise of a motor because of dammed-up sexual wishes and unresolved psychological conflicts. In the crowd of anonymous people a former girlfriend from school appears. She represents an earlier stage of my life. At the same time I become aware in the dream that my husband, my animus, is still not there, is still suppressed. And then I see a symbol of my youth, a wretched creature, a bundle of suffering, helpless, sad, pitiable in manner and dress, thus doubly pathetic.

The left side, that is, the emotional side, is inhibited in its development, and what is hidden behind it is so suppressed that it cannot even be clearly seen in the dream.

These dreams appeared to be activated at different times by the current theme of our discussions in the counseling sessions. The dream Nora has just described and interpreted appeared while we were discussing the problems of her youth. Those following occurred during the time we were considering Nora's childhood and asking what significance it might have for her later difficulties.

I was with my mother in the kitchen of our house. She was taking charge as if it were her own, and I felt superfluous. For this reason I went into the living room, but there it was ice-cold, inhospitable, and uncomfortable. A clothes horse which did not at all belong there stood in the middle of the room. I didn't want to remain in this room because it was too cold.

The shadow of my mother! Her image dominates the scene, the kitchen, the place where sexual and psychological "vegetables" are handled. No wonder my infantile identity seems to be out of place there, but also in the other life, in the living room, there is no feeling of security. The clothes horse in the middle of the living room warns me of the necessity to wash away the filth of my childhood. I still feel the coldness of that dream today in a corner of my soul.

I walked into a room. My mother sat at a desk and wrote. I think we talked for a while, and then I went away again. A short time later I came back and saw that my mother had fallen asleep at the desk. That seemed strange, and I shook her awake. She said she had taken sleeping pills. I had guessed something of the sort. I called to my husband who was somewhere in the apartment and told him he must immediately call the doctor so that mother could have her stomach pumped out. Meanwhile mother had lain down across a bed, and I stood before her. Then she suddenly laughed spitefully and said she had not taken any pills at all. I no longer knew the truth. I said to my husband, "You must telephone anyway. I do not want to take responsibility for this."

The title for this dream could be "The Mother, Her Fate." Of course, it would be easy for me to blame her for all my problems. I must be careful not to shift my responsibility to her. If only I don't make the same mistakes with our children my parents did with me! In the dream my mother is writing at a desk: The mother image is speaking to me. In my subconscious I come to terms with her. Does the sleeping mother mean that her image is no longer so effective or that I am again suppressing it, perhaps because it is laden with conflicts? However, my reaction is positive. The supposed suicide attempt indicates a weakening of the mother image. The mother complex must be healed, and I mobilize my animus—my husband—to call my inner physician. I am seized by doubt. I don't know where I stand with my mother and her image. I somehow feel guilty in regard to her—was Freud right about the Electra complex? —for even in the dream I will not accept responsibility for her possible death. The dream does not say whether or not the doctor pumped her stomach, but this dream and my mother are still on my stomach.

In psychosomatics the body is considered a psychological organ. Many popular figures of speech indicate this: A person is nettled when he is annoyed; he becomes green with envy; a problem lies heavily upon his chest; he faces a challenge with his heart in his throat; his breath is taken away by surprise; he feels weak or his hair stands on end when he is frightened. One does well to pay attention to physical symptoms in order to hear the soft whispering of the soul.

While the maternal influence upon Nora's development can be traced to a domineering, negative mother image, the father image repeatedly appears to correspond to that of her husband. Among other things, the following dream indicates this:

I stood with my mother in the middle of a field. It was raining, snowing, and storming, but we had no umbrella and were not wearing warm clothes. All around us stretched wide fields, but I saw no shelter. We were completely without protection. We were actually on the way to visit a woman physician whom I occasionally saw a few years ago, and my husband had promised to drive us there in the car. We had been waiting for him a long time. I looked in the direction we were supposed to go and saw at some distance an apple tree completely covered with pink blossoms. Behind it stood a somewhat larger pear tree with white blossoms. These trees in themselves would have made a splendid picture, but the violent rain beat down mercilessly upon the beautiful blossoms, and I thought it would destroy them.

I looked back and saw my husband riding up on a bicycle. I could not understand this at all. He rode in a great circle around us on the left side, and then I realized it was not my husband but my father, and he was riding my bicycle. I called to him that he would have to wipe it off if he was going to use it, otherwise it would rust. He advised us to come home since we only had to be at the doctor's at five. I believe that it was now again my husband who said this. My watch showed ten minutes past four in the afternoon. My mother and I decided to go on foot. We were having to wait anyway.

The open field probably represents the open world where I have to find a place. Has my childhood prepared me for it? The world is stormy and I am without protection—no umbrella in my hand, no proper clothing. No wonder I seek healing help—the woman doctor —in order to improve my life, but I wait in vain for inner support from my animus. My exaggerated romanticism, which often helps me in the problems of everyday life, is also seen in the dream in the apple tree with pink blossoms and the pear tree with white blossoms. But up to this time in the dream, and that means up to this time in my subconscious, the destructive, threatening storm of my childhood experiences and conflicts covers the splendid blossoms of romanticism. Finally, my husband appears, not as expected in a protecting car, but on a bicycle. There will thus be a slow and not easy development. And again it is the emotional side—the left— which is approached. That suddenly my father, not my husband, appears does not surprise me any more since I am aware how much I sought my father in my husband, how I see them as identical, and how I compare them with each other. I understand too why I can't really say yes to my husband. It's strange that he appears on my bicycle. Am I seeking sexual fulfillment with him in this fetishistic manner?

Fetishism is a perversion in which a person seeks sexual satisfaction through a symbolic object. Of course, there are also religious, cultural, and other fetishes, for example, money as a means to power, drugs as substitute for religion, and so on.

No wonder I also dream the word *clean*, for feelings of guilt exist when one wants to sleep with her father. His call to come home represents the attempt of my subconscious to take the road back to childhood in order finally to be free of him. The reference to five o'clock, that is, to a later hour, indicates my skepticism about the possibility of being cured quickly. That is why my husband, with whom I must meanwhile live, appears again. The slow maturing is also expressed by the fact that I now make my way on foot to the doctor accompanied by my mother whose image will probably never leave me.

4: Nora's Early Childhood

No one lives completely in the present. Indeed, most people live more in the past or with their eyes on the future. In recent years psychotherapy has centered on the patient's present, but this emphasis may arbitrarily threaten the wholeness of the individual. I rather believe that wholeness means one carries with him the yesterday of experiences, the today of daily demands, and the tomorrow of hopes. Certainly a counterweight must always be placed where the balance is disturbed. Depressives strongly anchored in the past need to extend their view into the future toward hope. A dreamer who wastes all his money running after the fata morgana (mirage) of an unattainable fortune must awaken to the sense of reality. The hard-boiled realist needs a romanticism which looks to the future.

While I spoke with Nora about her past, I tried to motivate her toward attaining a unity of thought and feeling with her present and her goal in life (Adler's basic life-plan). With Nora's permission, I reproduce the following sections from a written account of her childhood experiences which she gave me as an extension of the memories she related in the counseling sessions.

I was born during the economic crisis between the two world wars on May 6, 1927, as the second daughter in a laborer's family.

I have always been ashamed of this background although I have intellectually accepted the fact that a worker's calling is just as dignified as any other.

We recognize here a root of Nora's manifold difficulties—the lack of a family identity.

I remember very little of my early childhood. One thing is certain: I was often depressed. Perhaps the family relationship gave me reason to be. My father was often angry, and I was afraid of him.

On the contrary, the father image should awaken in the child a trust in himself, his environment, and God.

Also I never received tenderness from him. Neither do I remember ever having spoken with him concerning important matters.

My mother was pedantic. To her, neat rooms and shining floors were most important. She clothed us properly and taught us to be clean and orderly, but I never felt that she loved me or understood me.

The mother image should awaken feelings of emotional warmth, "motherliness," the capacity for devotion, characteristics which—as we see from the description of Nora's current problems—she thoroughly lacks, probably because of a negative, frustrating mother image.

When I was about three years old, I once sat on her lap, but she pushed me away with loud scolding when she discovered I had damp underpants. How was I to understand this world? I simply crawled under the table and gave myself over to defiance and rebellion.

When I was five years old, my mother took me to kindergarten. She left me immediately although the other mothers remained an hour or two. I felt abandoned and betrayed. I knew she had to go to work to earn money by cleaning offices, but I thought for once she could postpone it on my account. With a large white pocket handkerchief in my hands, I sat in the midst of many unfamiliar children. I was timid and anxious, but the other children—so it seemed to me —were confident and could immediately call the teacher by name.

Only on the way home did I get to know a girl who lived in my neighborhood. I made friends with her, and we remained so for the rest of our school days.

I remember very little about kindergarten except for a couple of experiences. On a splendid spring afternoon the class went out into the fields. I could take no pleasure either in the games or in nature because I was so afraid of going home that afternoon. At noon while my parents were away at work and I was alone with my sister, I had dropped some dishes and broken them. I was sure my mother's rage would greet me, but when I got home, nothing bad happened.

That same year I was to say a little verse in the church during the Christmas ceremony but got dreadful stage fright beforehand. I tried to tell my mother and father, but they laughed at me. So I learned that one always remains alone with his problems, that one is not understood. Fortunately I got sick before the ceremony and thus the conflict was avoided.

In the first three years of school we had an older teacher who was always sour. We were afraid of him because he was humorless and strict.

It is a shame that this teacher could not replace Nora's father as a positive image, but he only emphasized the negative father image she had received at home.

At that time something occurred which confused me. During bad weather I was hit and knocked down by a skidding car. My coat was torn and soiled, and I had a bump on my forehead, but I was afraid to tell my mother what had actually happened. I made something up about a fall on the playground. Soon, however, the driver came and explained. He was prepared to pay for all damages. I was surprised, for my mother did not scold me. That night my father bent down and caressed me. In my half-sleep this confused me even more. I was aware of it all, and the memory of his touching me is still painful.

Here the question might occur whether the father made improper advances to the child, or whether the father and perhaps also the mother were much better parents than they seemed to their daughter. From Freud himself we know that many grown women assert they were raped as little girls by their fathers, a fact which later investigation proved real only in the girls' imaginations. Of course, in regard to the subjective understanding of connections between supposedly negative attitudes of parents and the difficulties of their children, it doesn't make any difference whether or not they are objectively correct, but it might console parents to know that their children are not always right in their judgments about them.

The only man of whom I have a positive memory during my school years is my fifth-grade teacher. It might be that he liked me. At a class reunion many of my schoolmates asserted he was partial to me. In any case, I tried hard for him and became a good student who created no problems.

On the other hand, the situation at home was anything but tolerable. Father came home intoxicated, and mother received him with a barrage of abuse. Immediately after supper he left the house to find more pleasant company at a bar. Late at night he came in really drunk, made wild insults, cursed, and threatened to commit suicide, to which purpose he turned on a gas jet. Then he went to sleep on the kitchen floor, and mother brought him to bed, all the while reproving and insulting him. I listened to it all, holding my breath and feeling paralyzed with fear. At the same time I was ashamed because the neighbors must have been able to hear it. Then, at some point, the fighting stopped, and I could go to sleep.

After such an occurrence there would be a cold war in our house. My parents would not speak a word to each other for two or three days. My sister and I knew plenty of bitterness and rage from my mother, for during this time she would not launch a direct attack against father. She railed at him to us and swore to pay him back and get a divorce. At such times I felt sorry for her and wanted to help her. I stopped being myself in order to identify better with her. In any case, I did not want to disappoint her. Whether I was walking down the street or sitting in school, I felt inferior. Could people read from my face what was going on inside me?

As soon as peace was restored, my mother treated me as if she had never needed me to work off her anger, and I felt superfluous. The ups and downs of these occurrences were often repeated. In time I became so sensitized that any loud discussion in a neighboring room awakened fear and tension in me.

My mother's behavior was not accidental. She had grown up in an alcoholic home. Nevertheless she married a man she knew loved alcohol.

In the choice of partners, a compulsion to repeat as well as a need for compensation is often decisive. A repetition compulsion plays a part in the attitude in marriage. Perhaps Nora's mother may have taken on the attitude of her own mother.

Difficulties can also arise because the circumstances make gratifying the need for compensation impossible. Marriage counseling is necessary, not only to reveal the backgrounds of the difficulties, but to develop new patterns of behavior.

My father lost his father in his earliest childhood. His mother earned a living for herself, my father, and his brother by selling newspaper subscriptions. His childhood was grim. His instability may come from his lack of a father. As time went on I disliked him more and more. He was a weakling, and he disgusted me.

These statements sound similar to those Nora made about her own husband. Although William is not an alcoholic, his weakness subconsciously reminds Nora of her father's weakness.

I often wished for a father I could love and of whom I could be proud. Luckily he did not drink away the earnings he received in the factory. Whenever anyone asked me about my father's work, I was ashamed to tell the truth because I thought they would then also know he was an alcoholic.

Unfortunately, I didn't get along with my sister who was three years older than I and preferred by my mother. I often asked myself if I were really the child of my parents. At home I formed no deep relationships.

Nevertheless, home had a power of attraction. During a school trip I began to cry, seemingly without reason. The teachers did not know what was wrong. I could not tell them because I didn't know. Only when I was home again and had taken a headache tablet did I feel well, perhaps because I knew that my mother was near.

Children from threatening families develop a subconscious fear of losing their home, of having divorced parents. Even staying away from home one or two days can activate such fears in a child.

Once when I was on vacation with my sister at the house of an aunt in a foreign country, I cried until my mother came to get me.

Two years later my mother succeeded in leaving me with this aunt for two weeks of the vacation, but I was not able to spend a single day happily. I would have some kind of accident and cry and cry. I suffered constantly from headaches. This vacation left me feeling bitter. I asked myself, as so often before, why I was depressed and why could I not be happy like the other children. I carried a sort of burden around within me, and it became heavier if I left the everyday routine. That could happen even in going to the dentist, for then I was seized by a dreadful anxiety.

One time a game with my cousin gave me the idea of self-gratification. My loneliness and lack of contact with others naturally encouraged this tendency. Masturbation became a compulsion. It consoled me when I was tense, but it also awakened new tensions because it gave me a bad conscience which in turn became a further burden.

While childhood years often lie in darkness and it is difficult to demonstrate precisely their importance for later attitudes and later difficulties, the relationships between youth and adulthood are better understood. Nevertheless, occurrences also come to pass in early youth which in the patient's recollection are seen as causes for later difficulties even though this cannot be proved objectively.

In this context, Freud spoke of cover memories, remembrances which are given as explanations of later disturbances but which in reality cover subconscious experiences which are the real causes. Only a differentiated investigation—for example, dream analysis and associative interpretations—into psychical relationships brings the real backgrounds to light. Precisely for this reason a thorough biography and its discussion is important. As long as one concentrates on the superficial relationships—on the cover memories—the deeper emotions can continue to have unhealthy effects. A thorough psychotherapeutic work is—at least in neurotically affected marriage and family disturbances—comparable to archeological work in which the top layers must be removed before one can reach those lying beneath.

Puberty is like a railroad switching tower which aims the journey of childhood years toward maturity. Those who have been damaged in childhood have difficulty attaining a consciousness of their identity. Others achieve a high degree of development. What was the case with Nora?

At the age of thirteen I entered high school, and a new life began for me. We had two teachers. One had diabetes and liver problems and accordingly was usually in a bad mood, but I didn't like the other teacher either. He repeatedly offended me with his remarks. I became furious, but I didn't mention it at home. Who could understand me there? Fortunately I made good grades.

For the first time, I was interested in boys. The object of my affections was a boy of my age in another class. He knew nothing about my feelings because my shyness allowed only stolen glances. I daydreamed a lot.

Frequently children and young people who have difficulties in everyday life daydream excessively.

Even in my adult years I have often daydreamed.

When a girlfriend in my class returned after a long illness, she told me of her stay in the hospital. I wished that I could also be ill and experience the same thing. In my daydreams I imagined how I would be tended to and cared for in the hospital. In other daydreams I pictured myself sick in bed while some boys and girls whom I particularly liked kept me company.

In the third level of high school, when I was fifteen, we took a two-day school trip to southern Switzerland to the Tessin area. As always, I went along reluctantly. I felt inhibited and was afraid of the unknown, but when our train neared Lugano, I was charmed by the landscape. In the afternoon we went walking in the Cassarete Valley and enjoyed the vineyards and the chestnut trees. In a forest meadow stood an old stone church. It seemed like an oasis of rest and peace. We looked down into the valley where between the vineyards the picturesque villages lay. In the distance rose the majestic, high, rocky cliffs called the Denti della Vecchia. In the south, blue Lake Lugano shimmered in the sunlight. The entire southern atmosphere made a deep impression on me. I would have liked to remain there. On an evening walk through the little village where we were staying at a youth hostel, we got to know some of the Tessin young people. I liked them as much as I liked the area where they lived.

The next morning we were awakened early. I walked to the window. Before me lay the sleeping village with its romantic stone houses and the narrow steep streets; I will never forget this picture. It touched me so deeply that I could not look at it enough, and for weeks afterward I longed for this place. Even in later years I have been drawn again and again to the south.

In spite of these beautiful impressions, the feelings of depression and not belonging did not leave. When I came home and looked in the mirror, I considered myself ugly. I was discouraged and demoralized.

Before graduation from high school I had to choose a career. I decided on business.

In retrospect, a feeling of loneliness permeated all those years. Unfortunately, the negative impressions were much stronger than the positive. They overshadowed the occasional bright moments which, of course, also occurred. Among them was playing the guitar and also my girlfriend. Although I went home with her and felt quite comfortable at her house, she never learned anything about my troubles or my most inner thoughts. I was careful not to tell her, a well-cared-for girl in orderly family circumstances, of my inharmonious family life.

Psychotherapeutic or marriage counseling work requires much time and energy. Occasionally one has the impression that there is time for nothing else. Many patients live in a trance because they are so concerned with their problems and the solutions. The more they concentrate on coming to terms with their difficulties, the quicker is their progress. If a person is too taken up with everyday problems, the counseling work can suffer. No psychotherapist likes to see a great change in a patient's life—such as divorce—in the middle of psychotherapeutic work because the patient could be diverted from the "psychological" work.

On the other hand, the counselor must be careful not to take the patient out of his everyday life so much that he lives on a psychological island. In such a case there is the risk of anchoring therapy work in thin air.

For this reason from time to time I interrupted the discussion of Nora's psychological problems and instead spoke of everyday occurrences. What was her everyday life like?

I am a housewife, the mother of three children, ages thirteen, eleven, and ten. Our one-family dwelling has a garden which I plant with flowers and vegetables. For four years I have been a member of the school board in our town. In my free time I enjoy music and walking.

On Sunday as a family we attend the service in the local church. Scarcely do I enter the church when tears fill my eyes. Since I was young, church bells have upset me emotionally. I succeed in getting control of myself by thinking of something banal and diverting my thoughts. Last Sunday young Christians testified about how they became free of drug addiction by joining the Jesus people. Again tears came to my eyes as I thought about the family lives of these young people and identified with them. I had to bite my lips or pinch my arm in order to control my feelings.

As we were leaving the church, William whispered, "A dreadful service." I was dismayed, for I could find nothing dreadful about it. I believe my husband cannot sympathize with the distress of these young people. I fell into a bad mood and again thought of the gulf which separates me from William. At home while preparing lunch I asked my daughters how they liked the service. Their opinions differed. On our Sunday afternoon walk I returned to the subject of the church service. William explained his point of view: The church increasingly allows itself to be misused by such displays only to appear modern. Nevertheless our conversation relaxed the tense mood, and we returned home peacefully.

On a weekday, before I am really awake, I am invaded by all the cares and problems of the coming day. I think of a thousand things and am afraid that I will not be able to deal with them.

I am reminded here of a tendency toward compulsive thought which apparently Nora's mother also showed, judging from her behavior.

My husband must leave the house at six-thirty. He is an engineer and works in an architectural office. At seven o'clock I awaken the children and prepare breakfast for them. As soon as they leave for school, I begin the housework.

Once a week I do a mountain of wash. Ironing and darning are among my chief activities. And then there are the various types of fruit to be canned. Occasionally I telephone my mother although this is not one of my favorite activities because she still tries to treat me like a little girl. A fifteen-minute coffee-break gives a respite in my busy morning's work. I use the pause to read the mail and the newspaper.

In the afternoon I often visit a friend in the hospital or make some other visit. The walk through the corridors of the hospital depresses me. At home again I help the children with their homework. I think of the visit to my sick girlfriend. She still has no idea how I feel and think deep inside, and yet we have known each other for forty years. Everybody thinks I am a happy wife and mother who lacks nothing. They know nothing of my dark side, nothing of the great emptiness, of my need to be different and to have to stand apart. Many envy me and have no idea about my pitiful emotional life.

When there is a school board meeting, I am away from home for two or three hours. I have already done everything that needs to be done in a neat home. Occasionally I visit the schools and enjoy the activities of the little ones. This gives me an opportunity to go back to my own childhood.

At home I become upset when the children are messy. Theoretically I know children think differently, but I cannot change my feelings. The fact that I am secretary of the school board and must write up the minutes at home means that I am condemned to extra work. After an evening meeting of the board, we go to an inn, play cards, and drink something. It is very cozy. It is usually midnight by the time I get home.

Occasionally I visit with the neighbors. One cannot totally isolate oneself. Sometimes I hear of some suffering, and it disturbs me. Of course, cooking is also one of my jobs, but I enjoy it as I enjoy the housekeeping in general. It's so easy to think of other things while doing it.

Once a week I drive to the shopping center to buy for the rest of the week. The people I see there remind me again and again of my unsolved problems. Since I have been treated by Dr. Harnik, however, I feel more hope and consolation because I am not alone with my difficulties any more. I realize how very much I have mixed up everyday life with the past and with brooding over my problems. For example, recently we had to go to the veterinarian with our children's sick guinea pig. I was just as upset as the children when it died and identified so much with the sickness and death of the animal that I wept. I cried because all of life seemed so senseless, because I had scolded the children for not giving the animal enough care, because it is so hard for me to bear my own troubles and I especially feel them strongly on weekends, and because I am afraid of burdening the children with my problems. Often I go to sleep depressed.

Part of my regular routine is a weekly visit to the hairdresser. I have known her since I was young. The hour and a half spent with her is like a recuperation, at least since I overcame my fearfulness. A couple of years ago her mother was about to commit suicide but was prevented. By accident I came to my hairdresser's apartment a short time after the incident. She was very depressed. Since then we have been very close.

It is well known that "shared sorrow is half a sorrow." By concerning ourselves with the problems of others, our problems become more bearable.

My hairdresser told me about her childhood which, like mine, was unhappy. She has children too, and so we always find new things to talk about. As a hairdresser she knows many people and their problems, and so I hear all kinds of news about our community. To put it frankly, we gossip over coffee and the time flies. Afterward work is much easier.

5: Nora's Youth and Everyday Life

Counseling work brought to light many, in part forgotten, memories from Nora's childhood, from her teenage years, and even from her everyday life, not to mention from the marriage which was always the center of our discussion. If these facts are here systematically presented, it is for didactical reasons. In reality this picture came into being in pieces, like a puzzle.

From Nora's description of her years in school and as a teenager, I take the following excerpts:

> I completed my business training in a candy factory. I have forgotten the first day at work but not the first week. I did only monotonous and uninteresting jobs, all the typical Girl Friday tasks—taking care of the correspondence, for example—but the work which bores most beginners did not seem so bad to me. I even enjoyed reading the letters, but at the end of the first week I cried out, "I don't like it." I continued anyway.
>
> Two older ladies worked in the office, and they saw me, the young one, as an intruder. They formed a front against me and gave me as little help as possible.
>
> After a few weeks, I still had discovered no pleasure in the work, and I wanted to quit, but my parents wouldn't hear of it. With a heavy heart, I stayed on, thinking about the endless three years before me.

I would be lying if I said that for three years I experienced only unhappiness. Attending trade school two days a week was fun. There I got to know Edith, and she and I were friends for many years. Also during the apprenticeship was a three-week stay in the country. We were to help a farm family with the increased planting necessary for the war. At the border many farmers had been drafted, and there was a lack of workers. The people with whom I stayed were friendly, but I was homesick. My usual anxiety in unfamiliar surroundings was with me here too.

The approaching Second World War threw its shadow upon us. In 1938 the Germans marched into Austria. The question was being asked whether Hitler also wanted to conquer Switzerland as a partly German-speaking area. In the summer of 1939 I visited relatives in Germany with my sister, and I experienced firsthand how Hitler youth felt and what sort of mentality prevailed in Germany. On the farm next to our relatives lived a family with four half-grown sons who were in the Hitler Youth. They bragged at every opportunity that Switzerland would someday belong to the German Reich. We would then experience miracles, they said. If we entered a store without saying "Heil Hitler!" people gave us hostile stares.

We witnessed a terrifying event: An old man was beaten by a young fellow only because he refused to give the Hitler greeting. Our uncle, who in the security of the immediate family thundered against Hitler, was afraid of being reported to the authorities by his own daughter, who admired Hitler. We heard rumors about concentration camps; we did not know what was true and what was "atrocity propaganda." I breathed a sigh of relief when after the vacation we were again on Swiss soil.

By the end of 1939 after Hitler had seized Poland, we in Switzerland were mobilized for war. The National Guard left their families and jobs to be directed to different places for border guard and civil defense. Even though there were Nazi sympathizers and defeatists, most people wanted to defend the independence of their country under any circumstances. My father served several months of military duty.

In addition to my anxiety about personal matters, I now felt the pervasive fear of Hitler. The streets seemed strange because men capable of bearing arms were missing or appeared only in uniform. Older pupils were requisitioned to bring in the harvest. Blackouts were made official and maintained. Cellars were furnished as air raid shelters. Local militias were formed. The women's auxiliary corps was established. Groceries and clothing were rationed. People were ordered to cultivate every square yard of usable ground.

In this connection Christian readers might be interested to learn that the man who was given the responsibility of planning and rationing in Switzerland accepted the job after withdrawing with friends for quiet and prayer to learn whether it was God's will that he be called to the task. He attributed the perfect success his plan enjoyed to Christian obedience. I knew this man who was a close friend of Dr. Paul Tournier and who has since died.

Twice our country was in serious danger of being attacked by Germany. People were afraid of losing their freedom, and they prayed. In school we followed the advances of the Germans up to 1943 in the atlas. Switzerland was completely surrounded by the Axis powers. German propaganda poisoned our morale. In June, 1940, the Germans occupied France, and a force of forty-two thousand French and Poles crossed our borders to be disarmed and interned by our soldiers. Refugees threatened to flood our country. Many—to our eternal shame and disgrace—were turned away and sent to certain death. People said, "The boat is full." Air battles occurred between Swiss and off-course German fighters. At night we heard the droning of Allied bomber squadrons in neighboring areas. Occasionally they also crossed our skies at great altitudes. At first we sounded air raid alarms and opened the bomb shelters, but later we became less concerned and remained in bed, yet we always breathed a sigh of relief when the all-clear signal was given. Occasionally bombs were accidentally dropped on Swiss soil, and there were deaths and injuries.

This was my environment in my midteens. Like most people I asked myself the meaning of these dreadful goings on. How we thanked God when in May, 1945, finally, the bells of peace rang.

As everyone knows, questions of faith are among the most difficult problems for young people. On the one hand, the young person makes a complete changeover by taking apart what he is taught and restructuring it. On the other, he is capable of great enthusiasm, but the type of religious enthusiasm which occurs in youth can evaporate after a time. Nevertheless religious experience, as well as religious doubt, are of great importance for character development in the formative years. Nora gave the following information concerning this question:

> At the age of barely sixteen I was confirmed. For a while I also attended meetings of the church youth group where I found good fellowship. My girlfriend from school was there, along with other friends from school. But suddenly the meetings ceased to mean anything. Of course, I considered faith something which had a place in life, but it did not especially touch me. My mother had taught us to pray. That is the only thing for which I credit her. Perhaps at that time my religious needs were hidden by other more urgent impressions and feelings.
>
> One particular experience made me realize I had somehow become very different from my mother. During the summer that I was seventeen, I went with her on a week-long bicycle trip. We were in the fourth year of the war, and because gasoline was scarce, many people were bicycling. At some point we had to get off and walk the bicycles uphill. When we got to our destination, we were exhausted. Then we learned that a few days earlier the owner of the inn had become seriously ill, and the number of guests had had to be reduced. However, the lady at the desk offered to look for a room for us in the neighborhood. When we heard her speaking on the telephone in the singing dialect of that area, we began to laugh hysterically, but my laughter changed to convulsive sobbing. I yearned for security, probably because I was so tired and uncertain about where we would stay. Although we did obtain good accommodations, I didn't get over being psychologically exhausted the entire week we were there. I cried often.
>
> One day we were lying upon a grassy slope of the Alps, and I said to my mother, "I am so afraid that you could die. I cannot imagine how I could continue to live without you."

Freud called attention to the fact that in reality such fears conceal the subconscious wish to see the mother dead or to kill her. Such an assumption fits Nora who hated her mother and therefore felt guilt as well as fear.

> Another problem which concerned me in those days was that I masturbated. This became a real addiction, and I was helpless in the face of my desire which seemed to increase when I was with my mother.

Psychoanalytically this can be explained in a couple of ways. Perhaps Nora masturbated because she was lonely; she may, however, have been compensating for Lesbian feelings toward her mother.

I worried about whether or not I would someday be able to achieve normal sexual intercourse being so wrapped up in myself. I could not expect clarification or comfort from my mother. The small amount of sexual knowledge I had came from my sister.

Like most young people, I had inferiority feelings because of acne. To these annoying blemishes I owed at least my inhibitions in regard to the boys at school. Only much later did I realize that I had used an external condition as an excuse to cover up the real reasons for my inhibitions. In any case, I could not believe anyone would ever be able to love me.

While working in the country I missed one good opportunity for a relationship with Phillip, a boy my own age. He and I had formed a sort of suffering friendship. The circumstances in the family with which we lived were bad, and we were treated poorly. We complained to each other, but a close relationship between us did not develop. Perhaps that was not totally due to my inhibitions.

Is it accidental or does one instinctively seek opportunities to meet repeatedly with the same or similar circumstances which call to mind one's complexes and difficulties? Not only at home but also at work I had to overcome my antipathy toward alcohol. One of the girls was divorced and drank to forget her loneliness. Several times a day I had to buy cognac for her at a nearby store. By evening she was always totally inebriated. She then became either sentimental or aggressive. The boss forbade me to get alcohol for her, but secretly I helped her because I was afraid of her angry retaliation.

Twice I missed an opportunity to have a boyfriend because of my mother's strict prohibitions. Once after going to the movies I was followed home by a boy who had sat next to me. He took down my address and then wrote to me a couple of times. On the one hand, I would very much have liked to return his interest—I did not because I feared my mother—but on the other hand, his writing errors bothered me. The other opportunity to get to know a boy took place at trade school where a fellow student paid attention to me. Again I refused the friendship because I was afraid of my mother.

I passed my final exams with honors. That was at least something. Of course, I would have preferred some distinction in life instead of this distinction in school work.

In looking back over Nora's family circumstances, the tensions during the war years, and the fears and inhibitions which characterized her psychological state, one can only be amazed at how well she adapted to life. It seems that healing powers are at work which at most we only sense but cannot point to with certainty. Why one person suffers a total collapse of psychological integrity and falls into depressions and mental illness while another in similar circumstances "gets by" remains one of the many secrets of human nature.

Of course, there are times of crisis in a person's development when the psychological balance is especially in danger. The two great crisis periods are puberty and the change of life, but also before and after these stages there seem to be times when one is less resistant to mental or social problems. That Nora did not have a total collapse in puberty indicates she had good mental powers of resistance. In the next phase of her life we expect therefore no great upheavals but rather continued fear, inhibition, and longing toward fulfillment.

I was surprised to receive a good position at the end of my training. In the business office of the central secretariat of the labor union I was able not only to work independently but also to become very quickly the chief bookkeeper. I was not surprised that at first I feared failure; I was surprised to discover that I was completely capable of handling the tasks. I was also happy finally to be financially independent and to be able to do what I liked.

Although Nora mastered social tasks—first in the business world and later as a housewife—all relationships demanding healthy emotions and affections developed problematically. We are thus curious to know about her first friendships with young men.

On one of my first ski trips I fell and was taken in tow by Theo, another skier. As a result we dated several times. Theo was a nice, respectable young man employed in the same sort of work as I. However when I felt he had serious intentions, the relationship became difficult for me to handle. One evening we sat in a café after having gone to a movie. I looked at him from the side and thought, "I will probably have to give him up because I will never really be able to love him." If I had been asked the reason, I would not have known how to answer. Theo was really very likable.

Shortly after this my sister married, and at the wedding I got to know René, her husband's friend. He was best man, and I was bridesmaid. He was five years older than I and had a girlfriend, but he seemed to like me and we dated. I told Theo about my new friend. René, who had grown up an orphan, was eager to have a family, and I felt threatened by this prospect. When I broke off our relationship, no one could understand. Mother particularly pressed me with her accusing questions which only made me more obstinate. I was glad to learn later that René got together with his old girlfriend again and that they were married.

As a result of these experiences I limited myself to nonbinding comradely relationships with young men from the athletic club. Occasionally I also saw Theo, but he could only shake his head over such a girl as I who seemed to change boyfriends so often. Whenever I saw him—and this happened also after I married my present husband—I was ashamed to remember that time. It now seems to me I was immoral.

Once my girlfriend and I spent the weekend in a mountain hut with two boys. Nothing happened, for we girls slept together as did the boys. We had told our parents we were going alone. We were supposed to be respectable young ladies!

I worked three years at my first job. The atmosphere was good although my colleagues expected me to be active in the union. Politics was not in my sphere of interest. Once the boss took me with him on a trip; we were away from the office for eight days. I had a wonderful time, but despite the suspicions of my colleagues, nothing "happened." To be sure the boss was not very scrupulous about marital fidelity, but toward me he was quite correct.

After leaving my first position I took a job in the office of a silk factory. About that time something happened which terrified me. My girlfriend had loaned me a book on feminine hygiene. I was startled to read that excessive masturbation makes later sexual intercourse impossible. There in black and white was what I had feared. I felt miserable; I thought I had ruined my life. In despair I turned to my mother. Cold and indignant, she turned away and would hear nothing of it. What had I really expected? That she would help me? How could I have been so deluded? Later I asked a girlfriend what she thought. She only laughed and said it was all in the imagination. I could not really believe that.

Then I began dating a young seminary student who was four years younger than I. We went together for almost four years. He was genuinely fond of me, and that is probably why he had the courage to say one day, "You should see a psychiatrist!"

At a ski resort I met Werner, a young man I really did not particularly like. Maybe that's why I went with him—my dislike protected me from the danger of marrying.

Now Nora notices she is in flight from marriage. The reason may be her fear of having a marriage like that of her parents, or possibly she is seeking an ideal father which no real-life man can live up to. She is perhaps in pursuit of her animus.

One day we discussed premarital intercourse. "That is completely out of the question," I told him. "At least before the engagement." That sounded very virtuous, but Werner could not know that for me virtue was no obstacle.

"And if your boyfriend should leave because he could not wait so long, what would you do then?" he asked.

"Let him go," was my prompt answer. My attitude made an impression on him, but I soon lost interest in the relationship. I had not found in Werner what I was looking for, but what was I really seeking?

I always encouraged a relationship until I realized it could go too far. Then I broke it off. Was I trying to get revenge on my father? More and more I began to ask myself what was really wrong with me. No man seemed good enough. One was too stupid, another too young or too boring, the third too rough. This one had an unsuitable job, that one did not seem to be my type. In every bowl of soup I found a hair. Where would it all lead?

In the midst of a gallery of potential marriage partners, one man so moved me that I believed I had finally found a suitable husband. But this time there was a difference of faith—he was Catholic, I Protestant—which gave me the excuse to break off the relationship. What a pity!

During this period of my life I made a trip to Paris with my girlfriend. We walked for hours along the Seine, saw Notre Dame cathedral, climbed the Eiffel Tower, and strolled through the various quarters of the city. Once when we went into a bar where female dancers appeared almost nude, I felt a certain excitement. I asked my girlfriend if her feelings had also been excited, and she said no.

Shortly before the trip to Paris I got to know a young man with whom I petted. The relationship with him lasted longer than with the other boys, probably because of the physical involvement. After my return from Paris our relations intensified, and one evening when we were alone in his apartment, we slept together. It was the first time for me. I felt nothing and was neither pleased nor distressed. We had intercourse one other time, but again I felt unsatisfied. Soon we broke up.

After working three years in the silk factory I moved to Paris, the city of my dreams. Now twenty-four years old, I took a position with a family with four boys, ages one to five. The work was too demanding, and after a few weeks I gave up my so boldly achieved freedom and went home.

Upon arriving home, I felt at the end of my rope. Afraid of the future and depressed about my failure in France, I could not sleep. For the first time I sought a psychiatrist. I lamented to him above all that I suffered from masturbation. He consoled me and gave me a sedative. With that the case was settled for him. I pulled myself together and took a position with a bank where I became secretary to the director. It was as simple as that. If I could only have that playful professional ease in my emotional life!

In the midst of this crisis which had come about through failure in her Paris job, Nora asserted a readiness to find support in religious faith. She describes her first personal religious encounter as follows:

One sleepless night I had a remarkable experience. As usual I was sunk in despair when I seemed to see on the bedcover near my face a hand stretching toward me. I held my breath. Undoubtedly someone wanted to help me, and I knew who it was: Jesus Christ. Now I was no longer alone. I knew I could turn to him in my need. I counted on his real though invisible presence. Something new had entered my life.

If someone were to think this encounter led to a total change in my life, I would have to disappoint him. Actually nothing in my everyday existence essentially changed, but I felt—in contrast to the previous despair—a deep joy when I thought back upon that fateful moment. I could now guide my life by Jesus.

Nora's basic characteristic is skepticism, and her opinion that nothing was essentially changed in her life is probably an understatement. In any case, from the time of this religious experience she had no more relations with men until she "discovered" her future husband. Perhaps this entry of the transcendental into the darkness of the young woman's soul provided the decisive impulse toward a new orientation in the conquest of her fear of marriage. Of course, the process of maturing is not ended when the future husband is met and the marriage ceremony performed. Indeed one may even ask whether a marriage is at all right when there are so many problems in the courtship as there were with Mrs. Miller.

While the biographical facts concerning childhood and youth, including the difficulties in choosing a mate, comprised those conversations dealing with Nora's personality, when we began to speak of the difficulties in her marital and family life, we turned our attention to the relationship with her husband before their marriage. At this time—after months of practice—she had already learned to objectivize and interpret. I had the impression her emotional attitude toward her husband was going through a change for the better, but I preferred not to ask about it too often.

6: Diagnosing Nora's Marital Illness

In order to suitably treat marital and family disturbance, one must first make a diagnosis. This is just as proper in marriage counseling as it is in medical practice. Of course, many marriage counselors content themselves with a step-by-step discussion of the problems without placing great value on diagnosing the disturbances. Nevertheless I believe every counselor has a certain idea or view of those relationships which may correspond with the obvious symptoms. For example, when a woman complains about her noncommunicative husband, one feels the problem is with her if she speaks excessively, very intensely, and very loudly. Behind such a woman's compulsion to talk is likely a need to compensate for a childhood fear or an exaggerated need to communicate. If a husband says, in a manner which seems peculiar to an objective listener, that his wife flirts with many men or carries on sexual affairs, then one would probably consider him a pathologically jealous person with a type of persecution complex (paranoia) or with a jealousy complex or a neurotic nature or a person who had a loveless childhood.

The clearer the relationships between the complaints and the background motivations or stimuli, the more certain one will feel in treating the difficulties. For instance, if a disturbance clearly expresses a normal crisis of maturing, one is more hopeful and can meet the client more reassuringly than if very serious character anomalies of one or the other marriage partners are suspected.

For the most part, a diagnosis is not made at first although a diagnostic supposition can be made after the first discussion. Often, difficulties are treated without a precise knowledge as to what is really behind them because subconscious motivations remain subconscious. When this happens, psychotherapy cannot be employed and the marriage counselor can only guide and support.

Establishing the diagnosis depends primarily upon the client. The more he reveals of himself, the more the counselor learns. An experienced counselor may often learn more than the client wants to admit, but such "stolen" knowledge is frequently unfruitful because the counselor does not possess a police function and cannot "convict" the client. For example, Nora was shocked when I suggested that possibly she had Lesbian tendencies. At that time the treatment was in danger of being broken off by the client. It is possible in group therapy, above all through the members themselves, to directly tell a client about an attitude unconscious to him but evident to other members of the group. But this can only be done when the relationship within the group is quite advanced and has become capable of bearing such a procedure. In general it is better to wait until the patient himself makes the diagnosis. The counselor may carefully help like a midwife, indicating the way and asking questions. The most important are those perceptions when the client can suddenly say, "Aha!"

Now, of course, there are also test procedures which more or less objectively discover primarily subconscious causes of manifest marital and family disturbances. Which tests should be applied, the choice of test psychologists, and the measurement of the test results in relationship to the subjective evaluation of the case by the counselor are questions which can only be answered from case to case.

Various counselors often use completely different diagnostic terminology. The same case can be designated by one counselor as a neurotic fixation attachment to the mother, while another prefers to speak of contrast marriage. The first counselor sees the contrasts but emphasizes background motivations—the dependency on the mother for example. The second, though recognizing the psychological backgrounds, prefers to proceed according to attitude therapy and to eliminate the contrasts in the relationship. Just as every counselor must work within his psychological concept as long as it is useful, any diagnosis is valid only insofar as it helps the patient.

We now return to Nora's case, particularly with a view to diagnosing her marital disturbances. We shall follow Nora's description concerning her relationship with her future husband.

I met William for the first time at a dance. In one of our early conversations I thought a spark jumped from him to me.

Such sparks indicate projections which are all the stronger the more fascinated the individual is and the more suddenly the spark comes. The idea of love at first sight is decidedly projection-laden. Whether such a projection will be useful or harmful depends upon whether or not the further development remains harmonious.

Other favorable factors for a husband also registered in my mind; age, profession, religious preference, family, looks—everything corresponded to my ideal.

Soon, however, emotional doubts, not dissimilar to those which had troubled my previous relationships with men, again emerged. This time reason came to my aid and told me I could no longer avoid marriage. In order to be sure my new acquaintance would not reproach me later when he learned about my family circumstances, I told William about my childhood and youth at a time when our relationship was not yet firm and it was still possible to dissolve it. He did not seem particularly interested.

I had the impression he did not yet wish to have a firm relationship, but I was wrong. When I suggested we continue seeing each other but also go out with others, William disagreed. I went along with his decision.

I cannot say I was happy, for I still felt the old resistance, against which I could only fight with a determined "I must!"

William and I went for walks and met at cafés. If we took in theaters, movies, or concerts, it was always at my suggestion. When we met at his or my parents' house, I had to keep talking in order to forget the emptiness inside me. Something seemed to be lacking in him, but probably something was lacking in both of us. William had not had much experience with girls, and his signs of affection were rather shy and reserved. Probably he had inhibitions too.

After we had been dating for nine months, we became engaged. I was afraid my father would drink too much at the engagement party, but he didn't. I was nevertheless disappointed—William gave me nothing but the engagement ring. In his family giving presents was unknown. Our children were to find this out later.

There were other disappointments. While away in military service he wrote me very meager, short, and mostly objective letters.

In Switzerland every boy serves a three-month enlistment duty and then for many years a three-week duty each year.

Once when I brought him to the train station after a vacation, William left me standing on the platform while he spoke with an officer. I considered this ill-mannered. When I mentioned it to him, he defended himself with a countercriticism: "You're just too sensitive." Such a reproach made me feel uncertain, for I was sensitive. I no longer knew when my sensitivity was too great and when the behavior of my partner, which caused the sensitivity, was wrong. Later in my marriage when difficulties arose, I often remembered this scene and thought, "You should have ended things then."

One day, sitting in my office in front of the typewriter, I turned the ring on my finger and thought, "This evening you must break the engagement." But I didn't. That same day William received a raise in salary. When I met him that evening, he was beaming and said he only wanted to make me happy. My determination to send him away evaporated.

We had become engaged in March and were married the following October. During those months we tried several times to have sexual relations but without success. If only we had broken off then, but we hoped for something better later.

Buying furniture for our apartment was no problem because we had similar tastes and the same attitude toward money, but the closer our wedding day came, the more anxious I grew. My fiancé was of the opinion that a wife must obey her husband. I laughed at him. I was not afraid of that, and indeed on this subject no real difficulties ever arose in our marriage.

I have often been sorry that before my marriage my religious faith was not yet deep enough that I could ask for guidance. Buffeted and blind but perhaps not completely wrong, I groped toward the darkness of the future.

If Nora had come for premarital counseling, I would have probably advised her to break off the relationship. Just as the motto "Pass? In case of doubt, never!" is important to drivers, so is its correlate to prospective newlyweds: "Marry? In case of doubt, never!" At the very least psychotherapeutic treatment of the relationship would have been in order. This marriage was stable enough and fulfilled many functions, but who can deny it also brought trouble and frustration and perhaps even damage to the children? One often hears there should be a sort of trial marriage before people actually get married, but William and Nora needed no trial marriage to see they had set out on an arduous journey. A trial marriage would not have enlightened them more.

At this point we still know too little about Mr. Miller to diagnose the relationship. Because of family problems in childhood and youth, Nora's psychological structure made complete devotion and an emotional and sexual relationship difficult. She was an inhibited personality, tending toward depression reactions, and she was troubled with inferiority feelings indicating an inferiority complex (feelings are conscious, the complex is subconscious).

At first glance we are inclined to blame Nora for the marital difficulties. But from the few facts we know about William, we can fairly suppose that he is a weak, somewhat unmasculine man with little capacity for leading a woman. From experience we know that the mental problems of one spouse correspond to those of the other. A husband's attachment to his mother, for example, is only one aspect of a marital struggle. The other aspect becomes apparent as soon as the corresponding attachment of the wife to her father is recognized. If one marriage partner accuses the other of having some complex, it may be assumed that such a complex is also present in the accuser. It is easier to project something from the subconscious upon another than to recognize it in oneself. In therapy, however, one learns to know himself better, thus diminishing this critical attitude.

On the kind of splendid autumn day I love so much, we were married. It was the beginning of a long, sorrowful time, not, however, without rays of sunlight. I earnestly prayed God would bless our marriage. I felt, even in the church, how much I would need his help. I put all my troubles aside because I wanted to be happy on this day, but I could not rid myself of worry about my father.

My expectation that marriage would solve our sexual problem was disappointed. It was now obvious that William could not give me what I longed for. He could not make a woman of me, as they say. New anxieties arose. I reproached him, he criticized me, and things only got worse. I became so tense that sexual intercourse was impossible for sheer physical reasons. The gynecologist I consulted told me it was a mental problem and that I must be patient.

I was convinced the solution to my problem lay with William. If he were more masculine, more energetic, more experienced, and more fatherly, I could give myself to him. We had ugly arguments. We were disappointed in our marriage and in each other.

Years later it occurred to me that he could not satisfy my needs because I prevented him. I was seeking a father in my husband, and it was not his fault he did not correspond to my idea of a father.

In my mind I blamed the psychiatrist who once counseled me and the psychologist I consulted shortly before I met William. They had not recognized my condition in time, and paradoxically advised that marriage would cure me. Marriage as a sanatorium! How absurd!

Three months after our marriage I demanded a divorce, but William begged me not to leave him. "I have become accustomed to you, and I like things the way they are," he said. "Accustomed," he said, not "I love you." It was a bitter pill, but I swallowed it and gave up the idea of divorce.

I worked half-days in an office and took care of the house. Every morning I read the Bible and prayed fervently for strength and for the healing of our marriage. During the day I felt okay, but as evening approached, feelings of fear and guilt welled up inside me. Convinced I was now paying for my self-abuse, one night I confessed to William. He seemed to understand but could not console me. The next time we quarreled, he threw the self-abuse up to me.

Once after an argument, I saw him crying. That made a great impression on me, not because he, a man, was crying—why shouldn't men be permitted to cry?—but because he was crying on my account. Deeply unhappy, I also suffered because I made William unhappy.

While I repeatedly made attempts at sexual rapport, my husband, obviously intimidated, avoided it. Besides, he was a night person, and I was a day person; so it was difficult for us to achieve compatibility.

After we had been married about a year, we moved. I hoped the change would improve the situation, for we would be farther away from my parents. My husband drove ahead to lead the moving van. When I entered the new apartment that evening, I fell weeping into his arms.

I liked the little town. Often I sat on the hill where the town was located and looked down into the valley and thought, "Here one could get well!" But I didn't find peace there either. Soon I again sought occupation outside the home. Since I gave William so little sexual fulfillment, I wanted to contribute something financially to the marriage although we did not need it. I worked in the sales office of a weaving mill that made material for furniture. Often I watched the lady who drew the designs for the fabric and envied her. I imagined that had I such a skilled profession I would have been able to become healthy sooner or to have remained single. I was always seeking outer solutions for my inner problems!

In the marriage everything remained the same. Aside from the sexual problems, all was well until I flew into a fit of rage, criticized William, and threatened to leave him. But then I calmed down, and we continued in the same, old, humdrum way. Once William agreed to a divorce, but we remained together anyway. I decided to go to a medical counselor, but when he closed my case recommending that I be patient, I decided to accept the burden of my unfulfilled marriage and not rebel any more.

A year and a half later we moved again. Still, nothing changed in our marriage. Every new attempt at sexual relations failed miserably, but I continued to hope. I changed from my earlier active role to a passive one, achieving only more disappointments. I often wept. My husband would be hateful for days. From time to time I consoled myself with masturbation.

Three years later, my father died of lung cancer. He suffered an agonizing death, but I was not able to mourn for him. On the contrary, I felt a certain relief. Soon afterward William went for reserve military training, and mother came to visit. She annoyed me, for I wanted to be alone. For a long time I had been trying to become free of her, at least outwardly. Usually we kissed when we met, but I considered this an unpleasant duty I had to force upon myself, a fact she took badly.

As the years passed, I began to wish for a child. The lady gynecologist I consulted found that everything was in order, but my husband had to have vitamin therapy. In the fifth year of marriage I became pregnant for the first time.

About this time I became painfully aware of how much my mother got on my nerves with her obsessive neatness. At the same time, I chased through the apartment cleaning as much as I could because I felt her shadow driving me on. When I visited her, I suddenly feared I would lose the child by spontaneous abortion. I blamed her too for my sexual misery. Then the thought came to me that there had been no pregnancy as long as my father was alive. Only after his death did I conceive. I imagine that during his lifetime I had not wanted a child.

I hoped for a girl; my husband, a boy. On the way home from a checkup, I suddenly had the certainty it would be a girl. My intuition also told me the birth would be on October 4 and not on October 8 as the doctor had calculated. And so it was. During the birth I felt quite alone. My husband was away with the reserve. It was a girl, and I was delighted. When my husband arrived a few hours after Mary was born, he was happy along with me in spite of his wish for a boy.

Caring for the baby required a lot of time, and I was plagued by fears that Mary would be damaged as I had been. I was afraid of making mistakes in raising her. If my parents were too strict with me, I now wanted to be the opposite and thus fell victim to inconsistency.

A year and a half later—I was again pregnant—my husband was transferred. I welcomed the move because I would be able to get even farther away from my mother. Of course, I soon realized that I had brought my problems with me to the new place. I wanted to have another girl but hoped for a boy for William's sake. It was another girl. Again my husband showed no disappointment. One day soon after Ann's birth, I suddenly had the feeling I must have a third child.

Ann was about five weeks premature and needed extra attention. Unfortunately, I had to ask my mother's help for awhile. I was so relieved when I could manage on my own and she could return home.

Ann was restless but healthy. She cried constantly and kept me very busy. Often I thought dejectedly, "I have so much trouble and work with this child!" I valued her as little as I valued myself. I gave her care and affection, but somehow I had no more accepted her emotionally than I had my husband and Mary. Perhaps the little one was conscious of this and cried to keep me at her bed. Later when she became difficult in school, I thought back on these first years and blamed myself.

Soon I was pregnant for the third time. Again I hoped for a boy to solve our problems. How foolish!

Behind the thought that a boy could solve the problems might be the idea of making the husband more happy and thus potent. Perhaps, however, this is also an archetype of the biblical role of the man-child, the Savior.

Was it the wish for a boy that told me it will be a boy or was it real intuition? At any rate, I was firmly convinced that this time my husband would have his wish. Our son was born unexpectedly at home, but everything went well. My husband was proud of his new heir. After the delivery I had myself sterilized.

The housekeeping and the three small children were a great burden. I resented bitterly William's lack of concern. His help could have greatly influenced the climate of our marriage. From time to time I had someone come in to help with the housework. One cleaning lady, a thoroughly maternal person, was very kind.

Aside from one disturbing illness—a lung inflammation which naturally caused us concern—our little boy was quite healthy, and it did me good to see him so peaceful and contented. I had not wanted him for myself but only for my husband. Ann remained the most troublesome child. She ran through the rooms, dug plants out of the flower pots, scattered dirt across the floor, and attacked her sister, but sometimes she could be very amusing. Because of her brother, I had too little time for her, and I believe she did not get enough attention.

One day I drew up a balance sheet of our marriage and my life. I had gone from one hope to another but also from one disappointment to another. With each move, with each new birth, I expected a miracle. I now admitted I was playing a losing game. I could expect no help from William. When I tried to talk to him about my feelings, he felt I was criticizing him. In part, I was to blame for his attitude because my words often poured out in a stormy, destructive flood. He seemed completely satisfied with his life. In his free time he liked to stay home with the children. He was, as people often say, a good paterfamilias. At this time, however, he acquired a habit which got on my nerves: He would use baby talk. In the children I found it funny, but not in him. It strengthened my impression of him as a weak, unmasculine, infantile man. No matter how often I asked him to stop, he would not. How could he be so childish and self-satisfied while I was almost going crazy?

The children and the housekeeping kept me running from morning to night. I scarcely had time to read a book, and I was always conscious of an inner "have to" driving me on. At the same time I felt incapable of dealing with life. I shuddered at the thought my life must go on this way eternally.

I seemed completely unsuited to marriage and family. My bitterness toward William grew. Often I was unjust to the children, and I took out on them my rage against myself and my fate. This burdened my conscience still more.

One day I sat on a bench in the park and watched the children playing in the sandbox. A couple of lovers sat nearby absorbed in their affection for each other. "I will never be able to experience that again," I thought. Soon I would be forty years old—life had passed me by. Recently I had read Hemingway's *For Whom the Bell Tolls* and had yearned to experience such a love as that between Maria and Robert. I did not realize that I was longing to receive love, not give it. I became apathetic and was on the verge of a nervous breakdown. At night I had attacks of suffocation, and I was afraid to get up to see about the children. Such attacks increased when my mother came to visit. As long as she was with us, sexual intercourse was completely out of the question. During the day I did not really feel at home in this new city because I had no friends. Then I pulled myself together and resolved to give up masturbation, but this decision of the will was not realized.

One day I decided to see the pastor.

Before we go into Nora's experience with her new counselor, some facts concerning Mr. Miller's role as husband and father may be useful in more clearly understanding the structure of this disturbed marriage and family.

Indeed William was no child of good fortune. He grew up in modest family circumstances, lost his father early, and had little opportunity to learn to develop genuine relationships. Thus he concentrated on his studies and on his job and neglected emotional involvements which make possible a more deep, spiritual community with a marriage partner. What he understood by love, as he himself once said, was custom and comfort. With such a man, a woman hungry for a deep relationship, like Nora, naturally could find no satisfaction. The fact that he could not sexually assert himself may have been partly because his marriage partner was inhibited and—figuratively—"emasculated" him, but he must partly accept failure as his own "guilt." This William apparently could not do, for to admit it would have meant that he too needed therapy.

He was "unconscious" of his lack of social ability and "conscious" of his inability to give his wife a meaningful sexual relationship. Obviously he was solely interested in self-satisfaction. Even if he had had other experiences before her, his problem with Nora would have remained, for he would not have been able to give the other partners any more than he had given his wife, that is, nothing. He used his wife as an object of his sexual need but could just as little devote himself to her as she to him.

That the children of such a marriage are also endangered is obvious. Not only do fears and uncertainty arise in them from the unrest and dissatisfaction of their parents, but they also lack the opportunity to develop capacities for personal relationships. One would have to—if he were assigning grades—give the father the worst ones because in his emotional helplessness he obviously placed himself on the children's level and destroyed the polarity which makes dialogue possible. His baby talk symbolized this tendency. Nora's annoyed reaction was not only motivated by her idea of a masculine man, which William could not represent, but also by her instinctive wish to experience a partner capable of real relationship. His infantile behavior indicated how much he failed her in this respect.

What this family needed was relationship therapy. For practical reasons the children could not be included; William refused psychotherapy, and so all hope was placed on Nora. Did she get the necessary relationship therapy? Would it suffice to make something more fruitful out of this family than had been possible up to now? Can we —as Nora did—now place our hope in the wisdom and experience of the pastor whom she consulted? Let us listen to her story.

It was a damp, cold, dark November day, completely appropriate to my mood. On the other hand, the dim light of the lamp in the pastor's study spread a friendly and comforting glow. Dissolved in tears, I briefly described my awkward situation. He wondered about the possible causes and mentioned quite in passing that an unfortunate predisposition could be at work. "What do you mean by that?" I asked him. He avoided my question, and I assumed he was referring to a Lesbian tendency.

Such a tendency can be neither proven nor denied. It is possible that many people are predisposed to react homosexually when corresponding influences are added, such as too strong or too weak a father, too domineering or too yielding a mother, unfavorable relationships with siblings, and so on. It would be simple to say that a particular homosexual is the way he is through predisposition or because psychotherapy was ineffective or effective. But such proof falters in that not every psychotherapist practices equally good therapy and not every patient can be treated equally effectively. How four percent of the population develops homosexually is a mystery, and we must try to help the suffering homosexual to free himself from homosexuality or to accept it should therapy fail.

Heterosexuals should not disdain the homosexual. It is the individual that is important and not whether he is homosexual or heterosexual. Nora had a strong prejudice against homosexuality, not the only prejudice she had brought from her unhappy childhood and youth into adult life. In this context a correspondence between Sigmund Freud and the mother of a homosexual is significant, and I have included it in the appendix.

The pastor suggested that I attempt thorough psychotherapy with him. I immediately agreed. I would have accepted anything which promised even the slightest help.

The pressures of suffering of someone seeking counsel provide an excellent basis for psychotherapy. If a client comes to be counseled from other motives—for example, at the order of an authority or on the wish of a family member—the chances for recovery are doubtful.

I was surprised that the pastor concerned himself with psychology.

Relieved, I went home and told my husband what I had done. He reluctantly approved.

I had two appointments a week with the pastor. It was as if a door had been opened. His sympathy almost bordered on the miraculous —at least so it seemed to me. I could not comprehend that a person cared about me. He succeeded above all in taking away some of my guilt feelings. When he supported masturbation instead of condemning it, I believed I had not heard correctly. I was endlessly thankful to him for that. He counseled against a divorce.

I took this new experience with me into everyday life, but it also caused me to argue with the fate which had treated me so cruelly.

As long as I told the pastor my life story, everything went well. Then one day I stood before a gaping emptiness and didn't know how to go on. He tried to help me by indicating the way with examples from his practice. He did not mention the word *transferral*— as I later became familiar with it—but instead used the word *flirting*, suggesting I practice it on him. I was horrified. Now the pastor too was expecting something from me. I wanted to give nothing, only take, and I could in no way accept the word *flirt*. For me it was a light, harmless game without importance for my problems. Occasionally I heard the voices of his wife and children from the next room. I could not at all imagine how I was to flirt with him in his office while his family could be heard just outside. "I consider that ticklish," I said.

"It is," he answered.

Later he explained it was important to retrieve the missing father relationship to be able to react normally in the marriage. This disturbed me. To retrieve a relationship which had been disturbed for years would require many years.

From this time on my relationship with the pastor was no longer untroubled. There were hours when I felt quite secure with him, and I went home happy. On those days my feelings of peace and harmony were carried over to the children. How nice, I thought, if it would always remain so, but sometimes he seemed hard, unjust, and aggressive. I ignored it. My situation seemed so hopeless that it no longer mattered if he too oppressed me.

"It would be better to have an unhappy love than none at all," he said one day. I perceived reproach in his voice. The stronger his expectations from me, the more obstinate I became. My feeling of spite was considerable. Even if I had wanted to do what he expected, I would not have been able. What did I have left other than obstinacy? Anyhow, I heard voices or steps outside his office, and that inhibited my behavior.

Once he told me other women patients dreamed of having sexual intercourse with their psychotherapist. I had no such dreams. At that time I dreamed very little, that is, I did not recall my dreams. My wishes were much more harmless, childish, more naîve, but I did not tell them to him. Very faintly, however, a special feeling for him was growing in me. Once when I saw him outside the office and he greeted me laughingly, this feeling became so intense, it frightened me. Perhaps I should have practiced flirting with the man or whatever he wanted, but I refused. At the next appointment we were silent almost the entire time. I looked up to the image of Christ hanging behind his chair and prayed quietly for help.

From then on, the pastor let me know of his disappointment. He was convinced that my behavior could be traced to the Lesbian tendency. "One must simply live with it," he said, "we can do nothing about it." I was deeply distressed. Above all I was sorry for my husband who, of all things, had to have such a wife. When I told William the pastor's opinion, he consoled me, "Nonsense, you must not believe everything he says."

Because of my husband's job we had to move again, this time back to an area near my hometown. The treatment had to be broken off, and I believe the pastor was happy to be rid of me.

I was a long time in getting over what I felt was yet another rejection. Never again, I swore to myself, would something like this happen to me. Father had left me in the lurch, my husband, and now the pastor. He at least I could forgive because he had gone to a lot of trouble for me.

Ann made difficulties in the new town because she refused to go to kindergarten alone and to remain there. For months I had to go with her. Like me, she was afraid of strange forces.

The treatment seemed to harm my relationship with my husband, whom I often hated. We set about building a house and furnishing it. I also took music lessons and painted, always hoping to fill the inner emptiness and lose my unrest and dissatisfaction. I simply did my duty although there is scarcely a word I hate more.

It would be unfair to criticize the pastor's behavior without knowing him and his intentions. Clients often see their counselors quite differently than they really are. At any rate it may be supposed the pastor was on the right road in establishing a relationship with Nora which would have brought her a sense of freedom toward herself and her husband, but perhaps he was too impatient. A Lesbian tendency does not prohibit the possibility of building a genuine human relationship. If the pastor had really been (and this must not necessarily be so) convinced the case was hopeless, as Nora thought, then he was in error because—as Freud confirmed—even the homosexual can be helped to harmony, inner peace, and the capacity for accomplishment. And finally the responsibility for breaking off the treatment cannot be laid upon the pastor but upon the move.

Diagnostic and Therapeutic Considerations in the Case

To make a simple and popular diagnosis we can merely say this is a case of a chronically sick marriage between people who were frustrated in childhood and thus suffered from relationship disturbances. Naturally various other pronouncements could be made in a diagnostic sense concerning Nora's Lesbian tendencies, the strange proclivity of her husband to move so often, and the partners' mutual attitudes of reproach.

Subjectively, for the most part Nora feels unhappy, has inferiority feelings with a tendency toward depression, allows herself to be plagued by guilt feelings, and perhaps tends slightly toward masochism. William seems to take the marital difficulties less hard, perhaps because he misses the lack of relationships less and concentrates more on functional satisfaction in the marriage. Perhaps also he is a person who takes life lightly, that is, has something like a happy nature. The children have more or less happily adjusted to the structure of this sick relationship, aside from the behavior problems of Ann and the defiant attitude of Mary. Nothing pathological can be seen in the boy.

Would it have been better to dissolve this marriage? This is an idle question. The couple have—in spite of some approaches toward divorce—nevertheless remained together, presumably not only for external advantages. Like their choice of a mate, their continued living together was motivated by inner compulsion (according to Freud, the repetition compulsion) and by a need which could be satisfied by the partner and nothing else. If we begin with the idea that only a happy marriage and complete fulfillment on all levels are meaningful, then of course such a marriage would have to be dissolved. How many of them would survive? And who would guarantee the partners would be able to find their way to happiness easier after the divorce?

But in this case the optimist could be proved right. The stability of this family, their social adjustment, the almost never flagging hope of this brave woman, her will to improve herself and her marriage, her maturation, the care of the husband and father, the childrens' good grades at school, the love of the parents for the children and of the children for their parents, Nora's maturing faith—all this and perhaps much more may be put on the scales to weigh against the idea of divorce. Whoever takes upon himself to speak the verdict "this marriage is not worth saving" or "it should be saved" is trying to play God.

As regards the prognosis of this marriage and family, it may be assumed with all due caution that an increasing improvement, above all, in the work with the individuation crisis, that is, with increasing age, is probable. The attitude of the partners toward each other and toward the marriage may yet change but probably in a positive rather than negative sense. Whether the capacity for orgasm in sexual intercourse can yet be developed in Nora is uncertain. Her capacity for forming relationships slowly but steadily increases. Whether the prognosis would have to be viewed more pessimistically in the absence of therapy is scarcely to be predicted. In any case treatment is an advantage. It aims directly at encouraging the capacity for forming relationships by creating and heightening a psychotherapeutic relationship and directly at the mobilization of relationships capable of functioning in the marriage and family and concurrently at a subjective feeling of happiness. In this way the children are indirectly protected from further damage.

PART II

Classifying Unhealthy Marriages

7: Marriage Illnesses

The case of the sick marriage and family described in part one presents an illness of medium seriousness, the treatment of which requires expert skill. Similar cases occur frequently in the practices of the psychiatrist, psychotherapist, and the marriage and family therapist. In the general practice of a marriage counselor, they make up only about 20 percent of the cases. General marriage counseling deals mainly with broader cases, above all those not essentially a matter of deep psychological problems as with Mrs. Miller. Naturally there are also much more difficult indeed even incurable cases, some of which end in divorce while some simply continue to languish. Not every divorce indicates an incurable marital illness. Presumably most divorces occur in curable marriages, that is, most marriages dissolved by divorce could have been treated and healed.

Marriage is more than a contract between two partners of opposite sex. It is also more than a basic unit of society. Not only is marriage a functional organization for satisfying many human needs, but marriage and the family represent a unit similar to one of a body which is more than the sum of its parts. From the philosophical point of view, marriage is a puzzling organization that is so imperfect one would most of all like to do away with it. On the other hand, no one has been able, at least up to now, to find any other organization which can satisfactorily replace it. From the religious point of view, marriage is a mystery corresponding to the relationship between God and man and, in the New Testament, between Christ and the church.

A classification of the sick marriage and the sick family must take all these functions and aspects into consideration to be able to correspond to reality. Even in a very differentiated classification, however, an actual case of a sick marriage always appears in an individual light and does not completely fit the scheme of classification. This is true also for the typology of the individual. No person is 100 percent introvert or extrovert but only more or less introvert or extrovert. By the same token there are no pure contrast marriages or infantile marriages or neurotic marriages, and so on, but only more or less contrast marriages, infantile marriages, and neurotic marriages. This limitation does not decrease the real value of a classification which quite simply facilitates our access to the specifically individual and unique aspect of a person or a marriage.

In order to take as many aspects of sick marriages as possible into consideration, I will use two symbols—the body and the house.

The Image of the Body

Probably because I was basically educated as a physician, I like very much to use physical images to illustrate marriage and family disturbances. This practice is not unjustified. One hears, for instance, of marriage illnesses, of healing or curing sick marriages, of growing pains in marriage. Even the Bible uses such images. Jesus said that only the sick need the physician and meant that only sinners need the Redeemer. "The Lord is your physician" is another phrase from the Bible. In 1 Corinthians 12, Paul uses the image of the body to describe the relationship of Christ to his church and the relationship of church members to one another. Naturally his comparison between psychological and intellectual realities and the body is not perfect, but it offers the advantage of great vividness. Thus we speak of childhood illnesses, illnesses of the middle years, and illness of old age in marriage. These terms directly express something about specific aspects of the maturing marriage without the necessity of puzzling over the essence of the maturing process.

In medicine we speak of the body's constitution. Correspondingly, we can speak of marriage structures and classify disturbances on this basis. Similarly there is a correspondence between functional disturbances in marriage and the family and functional disturbances of the body.

Marital and Family Disturbances or Illnesses Caused by Outer Influences

In internal medicine and in medicine of the whole person there is a tendency to assume, even in illnesses which come about through outer factors, a certain inner receptivity of the individual to become sick or to have an accident. But in the foreground is an agent working from the outside. An accident is not pure accident; there is a certain predisposition for the accident, but outer circumstances play a great part. No matter how much I might psychologically seek my death in traffic, if no car comes toward me to hit me, I remain unharmed. That I am struck, however, is no pure accident; somehow I was ready to allow myself to be hit by the other driver.

The same is true for those marital difficulties which are seemingly due to stress, poverty, war, and so on. Because the marriage in and of itself already shows a certain degree of disintegration, it can become ill or die through outer circumstances. An outer separation alone—even if it lasts for years—does not necessarily lead to alienation. Nevertheless involuntary separation or poverty can cause such stress that one can rightly speak of external pathogens, or factors, which cause illness.

The following case shows a marital illness caused by external influences:

John, forty-five years old, and his wife, Martha, forty-two years old, appeared together for counseling. "We want to know finally what is wrong with our marriage," they declared. "We love each other and have been married for twenty years, but we have many difficulties that are usually seen only in young married people." While John had done border duty during the Second World War, his wife took care of the farm they owned. His visits home were infrequent, but during them the couple got along well. Only when John came home to stay did difficulties in living together appear as had only existed in the first two or three years of their marriage. Even the children, who in spite of the absence of the father had behaved themselves well, now became defiant, tired of school, obtrusive. What had happened?

During John's absence, Martha had assumed both masculine and feminine roles in the house and in raising the children. She did this very well. Scarcely was John home again, however, than she had to give up her accustomed role. Actually, this couple could have discovered the causes of their problems without a counselor, but they were blinded by their emotional behavior and each saw only the faults of the other. In one argument Martha cried, "Oh, if only you had never come home from the war! Things were better here without you!" Whereupon her husband disappeared for three days. He spent the time going from one bar to another getting drunk. Then he came to his senses, and his love for his wife and children drew him home again. Meanwhile Martha had also regained her psychological equilibrium, and she received John in a friendly manner as if nothing had happened. Some time later the arguments were repeated until it was decided they should come for counseling. It was not difficult to help them out of their crisis. As soon as they realized they had to rethink their roles, they succeeded in fashioning a new relationship. The children too were soon able to be content.

This example illustrating the importance of external influences and the origins of marriage illnesses is a marginal case. Fortunately, wars are infrequent. Apartment problems, economic difficulties, and unemployment are much more frequent threats to marital and family peace. The temptations presented to the husband by an amorous female neighbor, to the wife by an "understanding" male, the isolation of the children from the neighborhood, racial, religious, and other discriminations can trouble family life to the extent that the collapse of a marriage or family ensues.

The degree to which the environment is friendly or unfriendly effects the happiness of a family. How often children bring the outside atmosphere home with them! Some experts give external circumstances too little attention, and some overvalue them. I am reminded of a woman who was not satisfied either as a wife or as a mother and sought always, without success, to solve her problems by external means—extra duties at work, changing her apartment, and so on. I remember also a family that tried for years to create domestic peace but was unsuccessful because a mother-in-law lived in the home. When the mother-in-law was finally convinced she would be better cared for at the home of a cousin and moved away, her son's family achieved peace.

Who would deny that the spirit of the times influences family life? There are, for example, areas in Switzerland in which there are no divorces, abortion is never considered, and patriarchal relationships prevail. In other areas society has opposite standards, and these are accepted by most families. I don't believe a total restructuring of our society, such as social revolutionaries have in mind, would bring any great happiness for marriages and families, but I do believe social evils could and should be done away with by reform to harmonize marriage and the family.

To characterize the spirit of our times with reference to the dangers it poses our families, a couple of indications may suffice. Over-emphasis on the sexual relationship in comparison with the total picture of the marital community causes couples to make constant demands upon and frustrate each other. The overemphasis on sexual technique at the expense of psychological and spiritual factors causes sexual feelings to become blunted, and the cultivation of a pseudoromantic ideal love in the mass media makes reality seem insufficient. The relativising of religious factors encourages a practical materialism which as a philosophy of life must sooner or later lead to disappointments. Overcultivation of emancipation ideas and the corresponding individualism make the fulfillment of social duties difficult.

One must have a strong character to row against the currents of the times. A strong inner relationship to the partner is necessary to be able to escape such currents. Even Paul warned Roman Christians of the spirit of the world in which they lived by advising them to renew their character through subordination to the will of God.

The following case illustrates how a combination of the effects of inner and outer factors leads to a sick marriage:

Adam, thirty-eight years old, came to counseling and complained that his wife, Dianne, had nothing in her head other than pretty clothes, constant vacations, and entertainment. She obviously never thought about what hard work he, the breadwinner, had to do in order to earn the money she needed for her extravagances. In a subsequent discussion with Dianne, it turned out the problem had two sides. She complained that her husband had sexually and emotionally neglected her and that she had sought this outer substitute which acted as a thorn in her husband's side. Her pride had forbidden her to reveal her needs to him openly and directly. He had had eyes and ears only for his work and not enough empathy to guess her problems.

I wanted to know exactly how she came upon this substitute solution which was indeed hard to sympathize with. She was encouraged in it by her girlfriend. The girlfriend maintained that husbands are obligated to work for their wives. Counseling was successful in this case because Dianne and Adam had sufficient insight and will to recognize their problems and to work them out. Dianne learned to take an interest in her husband's work, and Adam mobilized more time and attention for her. Since the marriage was childless, Dianne took up childcare in the neighborhood and so developed her maternal instincts.

Among outer factors which threaten marriage are certain sexual deficiencies. I emphasize *certain* because most sexual problems are of neurotic origin and must be discussed in the context of neurotic marriages, but certain sexual questions are of external nature. There was, for example, a man who found the sexual act painful and avoided it as much as possible because he did not have the courage to confess his problem to his wife. She did not want to complain when he let weeks go by before condescending to sexual intercourse. Thus months passed, and the couple became alienated. At the marriage counselor's office, problems which already indicated secondary disturbances were discussed for hours. A simple intervention—a phimosis operation—could have prevented these developments.

Among other causes of sexual origin which can be considered external are faulty birth control practices. One woman, although she declared herself ready to use birth control pills to assure almost absolute safety, had an inner fear of endangering her health. She was physically examined by a doctor who found no reason to deny her the pill. A psychological examination was not undertaken. Had it been, her anxiety would have been discovered and treated. Under certain circumstances the pill has to be given up. The oversight was paid for by an increasing secondary frigidity as a result of the inner fear. Gradually a general marital crisis appeared because this pathological development occurs slowly and half-consciously. Marriage counseling had to slowly gather the thread of the confused situation until the relationship could be clarified and the defect removed.

Similar situations can occur with the use of other methods of birth control. When the rhythm method or the intrauterine device is used, the subconscious fear of undesired pregnancy (objectively justified because of the smaller margin of safety) can have the same effect as fear of damaging one's health with the pill. The use of the condom causes subconscious resistances of aesthetic nature and can lead to frigidity or impotence.

It cannot therefore often and clearly enough be emphasized that birth control is a subject of methodical or technical as well as psychological counseling and, in the presence of religious scruples, of pastoral counseling. The way birth control is practiced these days—to a certain degree out of a box or jar like candy—can only be lamented from the standpoint of the marriage counselor. Neither is it any wonder there are so many mistakes and abortions. Birth control to measure—that is, in accordance with individual counsel—is the correct answer to this great question of our time.

Bodily or psychological illnesses or defects can also be the beginning of a pathological development in marriage when the problem is great and the capacity of the husband or wife exhausted. Nevertheless it is astonishing how marriages often continue under the most difficult circumstances. I am reminded of a man who was stricken with infantile paralysis shortly after the wedding and for years had to be cared for by his wife. He was paralyzed in both arms and legs, and the sexual relationship could not be continued. In addition, his wife had to work to support both of them. Not only did the love of the courageous wife continue, but it became even more intense under these frustrations and burdens.

I also remember a case in which an athletically built man in his healthiest years often maltreated his wife. She remained with him only because she hoped to convert him by her prayers. One day the man fell victim to a cerebral stroke which paralyzed one side of his body. Since he was dependent on his wife, his violent character changed for the better. The relationship of the couple deepened noticeably.

I can add to these two cases which emphasize the heroism of the wife the example of a husband proving himself a "hero of marital fidelity." A childless couple had made a good start in marriage, but the wife, a very busy lawyer, began to drink heavily. After alcoholic excesses she lost her moral inhibitions and had sexual relations with anyone she could find. Not only did the husband forgive her indiscretions, he saw to it she was given treatment. The drama of her excesses and treatment with relapses and new treatments lasted approximately ten years until finally a complete cure was effected. It was like a miracle. The couple was still together and loved each other even more than at the beginning of their marriage.

Who, however, would throw the first stone at the man who entered an adulterous relationship with his secretary after his wife had suffered five years from multiple sclerosis which chained her to bed and made all marital relationships difficult? His conscience caused him to make great effort to put an end to the relationship, but his frustrations were so deep he could not give it up. Many people who knew the couple claimed he did not want to give it up.

Especially chronic suffering of the husband or wife can gravely impair and encumber a marriage. When tuberculosis was still a dreaded illness requiring many years in a sanatorium, there were great tragedies in family life because the couple was exposed to separation, financial sacrifice, cares, and fears, as well as adulterous temptations.

If physical illness is troubling for a marriage, the danger of marital disintegration is even greater when there is mental illness. Depressions and schizophrenic reactions can suddenly block a functioning relationship and present the healthy partner with problems which only too often exceed his capacity. I remember a case which at first looked very bad but had a good ending. It concerned a forty-eight-year-old woman who came to me because she was worrying about her husband who "has changed so much." He was fifty-five years old, had always been nice and obliging, but suddenly no longer spoke to her, neglected her sexually, and behaved peculiarly. It was not difficult to diagnose in this man the so-called involution depression, that is, a depression caused by climacteric changes. In our discussion he told me he still loved his wife—after all, they had lived together harmoniously for twenty-five years—but he longed endlessly for a child and thus was seeking a young partner with whom he could fulfill his wish. The man was successfully helped through this troubled time, and after a crisis of a year and a half the marriage calmed down again. But how often does "chance" lead to secondary complications and disturbance in a marriage which has been functioning well!

In many cases the boundary between pathological marriages which are structurally deficient and those which, although stable in their structure, are ill due to outer accidental causes is fluid. For example, an epileptic may have a normal and satisfactory relationship with his mate for years, but an essential change in the epileptic illness may cause personality metamorphosis that will seem unbearable to the healthy partner. This sort of relational crisis may also occur when a significant religious or philosophical experience drives a person to a new attitude with which the partner does not agree.

I remember a man who for many years worked responsibly as the manager of a garage; he had an excellent relationship with his wife and was also a good father. One day he concluded that life had no meaning and that the best thing he could do for himself and for the world would be to end his life (suicide of accounting). Instead, he began to drink, to lead a life of pleasure, and quite simply to allow himself to drift. This character change led to a serious marital and family crisis. The couple divorced, and the man degenerated completely. Unfortunately, marriage counseling came too late.

The birth of an abnormal child can place so great a stress on the family, on the mother, or on the father that the equilibrium of everyone involved is seriously disturbed. When people are unable to reestablish this equilibrium, the "death" of the marriage is often inevitable. Outside circumstances can initiate developments which result in familial and marital tragedy.

Life is so multiform and the dangers which threaten it so manifold that it is a miracle that existence continues. This comment can also refer to marriage and the family. This institution is so threatened by outer factors that we can only be astounded it is still around.

The foregoing examples can be termed cases of *marriage illnesses* since the disturbances originated with outer accidental circumstances. We will now direct our attention to *sick marriages,* those disturbed relationships which are characterized by internal structural problems. The differences between these two classifications correspond to similar terminology used in medical practice: Sickness attacks the individual from outside while a sick person is infected in totality. Of course, the boundaries fluctuate.

8: The Structurally Sick Marriage

In this classification are all illnesses which originate in the structure of the marriage itself. Of course, in practice external and internal events cannot be clearly delineated, but for didactic reasons it is advisable to consider marital disturbances separately. Frequently, the infirmity or the lack of viability of a marriage becomes evident only when outer supports are taken away. I am thinking, for example, of marriages in which the partners work together in a family business. No other deeper tie binds them than a common business interest. Scarcely is the financial goal reached when one of the partners, usually the wife, is excluded from working in the business. Then the marriage begins to fall apart.

In this connection I think also of those fragile marriages which originated from the partners' strong desire to be parents. Since only the children hold the couple together, as soon as the only child of such a marriage dies or the children grow up and leave home, the marriage withers and dies.

A marriage that is structurally sick is one in which a genuine personal relationship is lacking. I call these constitutionally weak marriages, for they do not evince one body but a functional relationship of members which can only exist as long as the functions are maintained.

Such marriages are often unstable from the outset. The decision to marry is characterized by doubt and uncertainty concerning the choice of a partner or whether one should marry at all. In retrospect a couple may determine that even at the beginning they had little or nothing to say to each other. Often they report after several years that they still consider the partner a stranger. Occasionally such people refer to their spouses as "Mr. X" or Mrs. X," not jokingly but in all earnestness. When there is a great age difference between husband and wife and the marriage obviously functions to satisfy infantile needs, the partnership may at first seem intimate. As time goes on, however, the two people increasingly become strangers. Of course, all partnerships based on projections, especially neurotic marriages, are subject to faulty development which expresses itself by increasing feelings of estrangement.

As opposed to medicine, where constitutional weakness can be diagnosed with relative ease, diagnosing a constitutionally weak marriage is extremely difficult and demands intuition and much experience. One must be careful in formulating assumptions concerning a constitutionally weak marriage because many clients who want a divorce are only waiting for the counselor to confirm their assertion that they really never belonged together. Indeed many people marry under the most unfavorable psychological circumstances imaginable (see *Risk and Chance in Marriage*).

If the marriage counselor determines that a couple is struggling for genuine relationship, he can greatly encourage them by pointing out that they have a constitutionally weak marriage and that their efforts at overcoming the difficulty are as praiseworthy as those of a weak person who is able to achieve great success in sports. Medicine assumes that one should not protect a weak constitution but harden it. By the same token the marriage and family body should be strengthened. This can be achieved by mobilizing new bonds, awakening love as a pledge of service, communicating new insights concerning the nature of marriage, setting goals of maturity or other ideals, activating the marriage and family members to reach out toward other people, and so on. The friendships of one or both partners can also help activate the capacity for relationship in the marriage if the friendships are in the context of marital responsibility. Otherwise they may threaten the weak marriage even more.

The constitutional weakness of a marriage can also be partial, that is, not pervasive at all levels. In such a case, stronger emphasis must be placed on the positive levels of the relationship to compensate for the weaknesses. The following case illustrates this approach:

Joan, forty-two years of age, complained about problems she could only explain with difficulty. Her husband, Dick, also forty-two, had a friendship of long standing with Charles, a man she could not like. Although her husband wanted her also to be friends with Charles, she could not follow the lofty thought processes of the two men, and she felt Dick belonged to her only on an intermediate level.

At the beginning of their thirteen-year marriage, Dick tried to introduce Joan to the mysteries of philosophy but had to give up because she was "ungifted" in this area. There was a time when Dick was satisfied with philosophical books, but then he found Charles, a man of the same turn of mind with whom he developed a close friendship. Their relationship so excluded Joan that she felt like a piece of furniture in their presence. She tried to suppress her rising jealousy and to console herself with the knowledge that the marriage was otherwise excellent and that her husband was a good father.

But a pervasive dissatisfaction dimmed her joy in the marriage. Occasionally she considered revenging herself against Dick by beginning an erotic relationship with another man, but she resisted this temptation. Conversations with the marriage counselor helped Joan see that even though the marriage could not function at one contact point sometimes imperfections must be accepted to prevent something worse. Dick began to realize how very much Joan hurt when she could not share with him the world in which he often felt most comfortable. He was able to sympathize with her in this problem. This couple attained a new solidarity of responsibility and feeling which enabled them to adjust their faulty relationship on the level of the intellectual.

Examples of such cases can be multiplied if we add to relationships with intellectual deficiencies those with philosophical or religious ones. Love is considered the main basis of marriage in our culture, but another important factor is often overlooked—intellectual harmony. Because one's outlook on life represents a basic characteristic of human existence, sooner or later dissatisfaction will develop if there are no intellectual bridges between husband and wife. Such marriages are by nature constitutionally weak and are susceptible to further disturbances and illnesses.

Childlessness can also be the basis for a structurally sick marriage. Intentional childlessness may indicate that either one or both of the spouses has deep psychological problems which irritate the marital structure, or it may indicate that the couple has an egocentric attitude toward life. However, a conscious decision not to have children can also be a responsible choice when it is made on genetic grounds, that is, a fear of passing on to children unhealthy physical or mental characteristics. Involuntary childlessness caused by the sterility of a spouse occurs in only about 10 percent of marriages.

Just as a tree expresses itself fully when it brings forth blossoms and fruit, so a marriage is fundamentally fulfilled when it produces children. Children are not additional partners to the marriage contract but constitutional elements in the family structure, foreseen in the marital plan. For example, if an average man were to build a house, he might attach shingle to shingle and board to board and so produce a tolerable little shack. But the construction of a comprehensive building is only possible when an architectural plan is made in advance, each room having its proper place in relationship to the whole. The toilet should hardly be placed in the immediate vicinity of the dining room, and the study of a father who is a teacher should not be next to the children's room.

In the same sense, children born into a marriage which had not preplanned their presence might be a source of happiness and might become part of a quite acceptable family hut. However, they could be entirely unwanted and tolerated as a burden that somehow does not belong in the family structure. A well-understood family plan—not just a birth control plan defined by numbers—is given to a couple by the creator. The family is a totality in which individuals have the right, even the duty, to mature personally and to fulfill themselves. At the same time they exist as parts of the whole with responsibility to one another and to the whole.

It is well known that illness can be more easily recognized and defined than health. Sick families are easier to recognize than healthy families. Today's family therapy owes its existence to the recognition of the totality of family design. For instance, one family member may attract the most attention—alcoholic father, neglected mother, thieving son, prostitute daughter, schizophrenic daughter, neurotic father, and so on—but such an obviously sick person only bears the symptoms of the sick family.

As a body functions less well when one part is missing, a marriage functions less well when the part represented by children is lacking. The assertion that childless marriages can become sick is to be understood in this sense.

When years go by and the family plan is still on the drawing board of God, difficulties on the sexual level usually appear, normally in the form of sexual indifference. It is as if the sexual centers said to each other, "It is all very fine that my master [mistress] is having a good time and obtains a deeper emotional relationship when he [she] sleeps with his [her] mate, but where are the visible fruits of this union, those recognizable by society? Aha! They've been omitted. Well, fine. Then we will not cooperate any more." It's a shame that such a conversation of our brain centers cannot be made audible, for it introduces boredom and emptiness into everyday life. The couple begins to glance longingly at fathers and mothers with their children. Their dreams indicate an incipient complex, and their temptations to adulterous relationships become stronger. One day it's all over for this tree, which in the beginning blossomed but remained without fruit.

At best paternal or maternal feelings are transferred to the spouse, and the relationship of partners becomes restructured into a child/father or child/mother relationship. A childless couple often achieves a relationship similar to the typical marriage relationship of individuals differing widely in age. The maturing process of the couple and of the marriage as a whole is blocked, and dissatisfaction and other symptoms of the sick marriage result.

The marriage made sick by childlessness can be healed when the relationships are made clear to the couple and when the couple can be motivated to sublimate their parental frustrations. Several healthy avenues are available such as adoption, caring for foster children, and involvement in community childcare programs. However, adopting a child solely for the purpose of helping heal a sick marriage is irresponsible.

I remember a couple who came to me shortly before their divorce was to be final. I was supposed to prepare them for it. Three years before after having been childless for many years, they had adopted two Vietnamese children. An observant marriage counselor could have perceived the internal decline of the relationship at that time, but obviously the couple had not accurately diagnosed their difficulties. They seized upon the opportunity to adopt children, feeling that would solve their problems. For a while the marriage blossomed, but then it relapsed more seriously into a crisis which led inevitably to divorce.

Such an adoption should take place only when the onset of marital disturbance can be traced to childlessness, and it is up to the marriage counselor to determine this.

If the large family was essentially more stable than the modern small family, it was not only because of functional reasons—economics, a sense of dignity, group consciousness. A large family has the possibility for a richer area of relationships and for the "more comfortable building complex" of the family structure.

In our cultural milieu we cannot achieve the large family based upon the bonds of consanguinity. We could, however, allow ourselves to be integrated as members of a group of people who live in the same building or neighborhood, of a church family, or of a foster family. In old Israel the individual understood himself to be part of a natural family, a member of the great family Israel, and a part of a nation consecrated by its God Yahweh. In the New Testament similar endeavors are also seen in the description of communal life. "And all who believed were together and had all things in common" (Acts 2:44). Community groups are an adequate solution for the needs of the isolated small family and are at the same time an aid for the problems of the childless marriage.

If a marriage is forced by the expectation of a child, it risks structural deficiency. Of course, the time is passed when a pregnant girl must marry the father of the child she is carrying, but a couple often decides to marry only or mainly because "the child should have a father." Under such circumstances marriage is viable only when sufficiently firm bonds are already present. In addition, the danger exists that children of such marriages will be rejected because the parents blame them for having to get married.

Frequently in the forced marriage resentments toward the partner develop because he or she is blamed for the undesired pregnancy. In spite of a good structure, the marriage can become ill. Sooner or later an attitude of reproach undermines the foundations of the marriage and a gulf forms between the partners.

In spite of the fact that statistics giving the forced marriage a bad prognosis are based on generalizations and do not allow for individual differences, some authorities believe that a forced marriage absolutely cannot be successful. People who are easily influenced by such pronouncements may constantly imagine that their marriage is not going well until it finally really begins to break down.

A special danger in the forced marriage is that problems which existed prior to the marriage will be pushed into the background. The undesired pregnancy must be dealt with first, but if underlying difficulties are not resolved, they will most certainly reappear to burden an already stressful situation. A common example of this is a religiously mixed forced marriage.

If the forced marriage involves young people—as is often the case —exaggerated expectations produce early disappointments and initiate early crises.

As an illustration, there was a chronically protracted case of marital sickness for which I had to give the expert opinion in a court case. It concerned Kathy and Joe, a couple who had had a difficult marriage for eight years, which supposedly had only been brought about by an undesired pregnancy. At first the couple, who had a high standard of living, tried to make the best of their marriage, but they soon discovered that they lacked the strength of will to realize such a decision. They probably would have had more success had they sought counseling at the beginning of their marriage. When they finally came for help, the marriage was totally on the rocks, and the chances of saving it remote.

Joe was thirty-two years old, Kathy thirty-four. They had only one child. A second pregnancy was not carried full term but was interrupted. I gave the court the following opinion:

Kathy appeared at my office and bitterly told of her experiences in the latter years of their marriage. She considered the marriage beyond hope and had come to me only on instructions of the judge who had ordered the couple to see a marriage counselor.

After knowing each other a short time—a relationship based

primarily on sexual attraction—Kathy had become pregnant and she and Joe had married. Soon after the wedding the difficulties began. Joe accused his wife of having tricked him. She despised him because he was tied to his mother's apron strings and did not know how to behave as a man. Although Joe supported the family, he contributed little to family life. Their frequent quarrels were repeatedly reconciled in bed. Joe's mother constantly interfered in the marriage of her only child. She had raised him alone since he was ten years old when his father died.

From time to time Joe and Kathy had separated to see how their feelings would develop and in the always illusory hope that after resuming the relationship things would improve. For long periods of time they lived together while each carried on extramarital affairs. Now their patience was at an end, and they wanted a divorce.

Joe chastised his wife for being willful and domineering and said she had appropriated his male role as head of the family. He admitted he had no deep feelings for her although he had valued her for years as a good sexual partner. He accepted the child, but Kathy undermined his authority to the extent that even his relationship with the child was in jeopardy. He was convinced that Kathy was only interested in continuing the marriage for financial reasons. In spite of the fact that she didn't love him, she was jealous. To escape the inferno at home, he had gone out a lot. He also wanted the divorce.

In a discussion with the two together Kathy declared that her husband was entirely to blame for the ruined marriage. Joe allowed this to pass without a retort but criticized her domineering manner and her self-righteousness. I recommended that the couple immediately stop the reproaches at home and limit themselves to a courteous relationship, but there was no improvement and no change. Subsequently I had private sessions with each spouse to see if either could be motivated to make another attempt at the marriage and to see if possible uncultivated feelings could be mobilized. They often did not keep appointments, and in my opinion the divorce cannot be prevented. This is a case of strongly contrasting partners who lack the capacity for adaptation. The marriage had little viability because no common interests and relationships outside the sexual bond existed. After the sexual charms had attenuated, attempts at relating on other levels failed. The child did not bind the parents but stood in the middle of their struggle for power. Kathy's domineering attitude, Joe's weakness, and his mother's intrusions combined to make the marriage even more difficult.

While domineering attitudes can make a marriage sick, a marriage can be considered sick from the beginning if it is characterized by strong contrasts. I call such a marriage a "high voltage marriage." It is recognizable in the premarital relationship, for even then the two people do not get along and doubt arises concerning the correctness of marriage.

The strong polarity between those involved is felt as unpleasant tension. They are on "pins and needles." Unrest characterizes the marriage and the couple, and the children do not know where they stand with their parents. Nevertheless, in many cases love can be present although the quarreling has either changed or killed tender feelings. If there is a divorce, the struggle often continues for years as the children are pulled back and forth.

The high voltage marriage is nevertheless well suited to dialogue therapy. The conversation in which contrasts are brought out is effective even if it brings no solutions, for the marriage counselor catalyzes the dialogue to avoid all too-violent explosions. Dialogue operates symbolically by representing the relationship between the extreme poles. It also defines the relationship in general. Through dialogue, fear and tension are dismantled, and an understanding of the partner's motivations is promoted. Dialogue therapy makes it possible for those involved in conflict to change their ingrained conditioned behavior and to control their reactions.

Occasional separations over one or two days can lessen the potential for tension. Such relief therapy is often indispensable when the capacity of one partner gives out and signs of nervousness or depression become apparent.

Well-intentioned groups of couples, family get-togethers, and discussions among two or three couples also offer the opportunity for releasing tensions when there is strong polarity. If a couple can succeed in taking part in service to their community, indirect decreases in the high tension of their personal relationship can occur.

Even when a high voltage marriage becomes bearable through good adaptation, the antagonism lasts into old age. In time the couple gets used to the fact that they think, speak, and act differently, but as long as they accept it, it doesn't bother them. On the contrary, in time they find they have an interesting relationship. They are the least in danger of having a boring marriage!

In contrast a low voltage marriage is characterized by an unusual assimilation of contrasts. The partners' characters or temperaments are predominantly identical, and their relationship lacks tension. In it there is boredom from the beginning in contrast to the boredom which only arises in the course of years when partners grow away from each other.

What leads people to prefer a partner with the same personality? Occasionally it's the fear of a high voltage marriage such as one's parents had. One may also need the security of knowing there will be no arguing in the marriage. In some cases a person is actually resistant to the sort of emotional maturing that can come about only in a tense relationship. Perhaps also there is an exaggerated narcissistic need to see one's characteristics reflected in the partner. Insofar as it is a marriage of convenience, the low voltage marriage quite simply expresses the lack of personal preference in the realm of common interests.

In practice one must distinguish between primary and secondary low voltage marriages. The latter type is a result of a chronically disturbed relationship. For example, a marriage may become gradually boring because one of the partners is too involved professionally and neglects the personal relationship. Or a partner may engage in a personal relationship outside the marriage so that gradually the marital relationship weakens.

While in the high voltage marriage dialogue can have a favorable influence, it is useless in the low voltage marriage. Here one must mobilize other possibilities. If the spouses are willing to be faithful and to recognize their responsibility for the marriage, a friendship with another couple who are in polar contrast to the low voltage couple can be helpful. Of course, one must awaken and encourage all those common interests that could make the marriage more exciting. If in strong contrast relationships a warning should be given before marriage because it is not known if the couple can handle their differences, such a warning is certainly called for when the partners already recognize the boredom of their relationship before marriage.

A second marriage can but doesn't have to become structurally sick. Experience teaches us that the second (or third) marriage can go better or worse than the earlier one(s), depending on the circumstances. If the earlier partner cannot be forgotten, then his or her shadow lies between the newly marrieds and prevents genuine communication. Often people do not learn from their earlier mistakes and repeat them in the new marriage. Of course, previous failure can serve as an impulse to improve in the second marriage, but good intentions do not always succeed.

The success of a second marriage also depends on whether the partner or partners are widowed or divorced. Widowed people tend to idealize their deceased partner and make the adaptation difficult by a too strong projection and by an attitude of expectation. Divorced people are in danger of proving to themselves and to their environment that they were "innocently" divorced; therefore they may develop a pharisaical attitude by thinking that they now must not have any more faults. Age may also play a role in determining the quality of a second marriage. A marriage in later years requires more difficult adaptation than a marriage in the younger and middle years.

Finally, the success of a second marriage depends upon whether there are children from the first marriage, how many, their ages, and whether or not children will be born into the second marriage.

When it becomes ill, the second marriage shows a variety of symptoms in which the real problems mix with the false and backgrounds are hidden by pretenses. Here are a few examples:

After a short period of mourning, a thirty-two-year-old widower, Art, married Judy, a twenty-eight-year-old woman from the office where he worked. The courtship did not last long because Art needed a mother for Heather, his daughter from the first marriage. Judy got along very well with eight-year-old Heather. Art had known his first wife from youth, and it had been a very good marriage. Before her death from an infection, she had made him promise to marry again as soon as possible. His fellow workers consoled him as well as they could, but Judy was able to do this best. A recent relationship had ended because the man had broken off with her. In addition, she was attracted to the role of mother.

The first month of marriage went by without visible disturbance although Judy often had to suppress annoyance. For example, a photograph of the deceased wife hung in the bedroom, and out of respect for the departed Art wanted everything in the house to be exactly as it had been before. Often in his conversations with Heather, he would use the following expressions: "Do you remember how it was when your mommy and I and you . . ." or "What would your mommy say now if . . ." This made Judy feel shut out of the relationship with her husband; she often felt as if she was merely playing the role of housekeeper.

Constantly aware of her deceased predecessor's shadow, Judy became upset and made mistakes. Without first asking Art, she removed the photograph of her invisible rival from the bedroom and placed it in Heather's room. Her husband reproached her and accused her of jealousy and lack of respect. Some days later when Judy corrected Heather, the little girl reacted as aggressively as her father: "Mama always allowed it."

For this Heather got a slap which was really meant for the deceased. "I am in charge here, and I am your mother now!" said Judy. Soon thereafter Heather became loud and obstinate at school, and the school psychologist, who supposed there was a problem with the stepmother, advised marriage counseling.

Luckily Art was able to realize that he had done neither the child nor himself a favor by marrying so soon after the death of his wife. Above all he had to recognize that it was a harsh disservice to Judy to make her live on the edge of the "marriage and family" he had first founded. It was also made clear to him that the most ideal stepmother has a much more difficult time in raising children than the real mother, not only because the latter has built up a relationship to the child from the beginning, but also because there is a widespread prejudice against stepmothers (vide fairy tales!).

Art changed his behavior, and Judy emerged from her defiant attitude. She saw that she had imagined her task as "mother of the orphan child and consolation of the widower" as too easy. She regretted having used the child as a scapegoat against her shadow rival and consciously came to terms with the stepmother situation. The marriage calmed down and consolidated, and when the family was blessed with a second child, everyone's happiness, including Heather's, was complete. In this case the couple could also be addressed in religious terms, and they recognized that service to God begins with service to one's fellow man.

The treatment went less smoothly in the next case:

Whitney, fifty years old, had been married a second time for five years to Margaret, a forty-five-year-old woman who had never been married before. Two years after the death of his first wife he decided on a second marriage to offer a real home to his teenage children, a fifteen-year-old boy and a fourteen-year-old girl. The first marriage was rather bad, and Whitney was afraid of a second marriage. The courtship lasted rather long because Whitney was afraid to introduce Margaret to the children. But one day the unavoidable occurred, and the children got to know and love the prospective stepmother and gave their blessing to the father's remarriage.

Scarcely had the adults married than the teenagers began to try to drive a wedge between their father and their stepmother. Their attempts were all the more successful because Whitney was soft and weak and could not control the children. Although Margaret tried everything possible to save the peace, she could no longer put up with the humiliations and left because Art would not stand up for her. The relationship of the couple was continued outside the home, and after the children moved away some years later, the couple achieved a "complete marriage."

The reverse situation, in which a widow with children marries for the second time, leads as a rule to less acute difficulties. Of course, in practice one also sees cases in which the only son of a widow seeks to supplant the stepfather. This can lead to insurmountable difficulties for the mother. For the most part, however, the son must give way to the power of the stepfather, whereby at least an external solution results. One can imagine, however, how it must feel to a mother who is forced to sacrifice her son from the first marriage for the peace of the second marriage.

The second marriage of divorced people presents special psychological problems. The tendency to avoid earlier mistakes by a compensatory attitude has already been mentioned. For the most part, earlier mistakes are repeated because most people are inclined to marry the same type of person again. According to the psychological studies of Leopold Szondi, people are attracted to others of the same genetic structure. Naturally, the second marriage of divorced people is also complicated by the presence of children from the first marriage. The relationship of the father or mother to the divorced partner is indirectly maintained by the right of visitation and child support. Frequently a tug of war between the divorced couple also burdens the relationship to the second partner. In such a marriage, as in the second marriage of one who is widowed, the shadow of the earlier partner can prevent unity.

To be able to reach as many divorced people as possible and to counsel them in a general way in their new life situation, I published a leaflet which was distributed in many areas in Switzerland. I have included it in the appendix of this book.

In addition to marriage at an early age or just before or during the change of life (climacteric), incongruency of age also presents a special danger. This classification would apply to a marriage in which the man is more than ten years older than the woman or one in which the woman is more than five years older than the man. Not only neurotic elements but also attitudinal defects can lead to a sick marital structure. The younger the younger partner in the marriage, the greater the risk of disappointments, while partners of middle and older age have a better chance for a successful marriage when there is a disparity of ages. The success of a marriage in which there is a great age difference essentially depends upon the partners' firmness of character. On the other hand, what causes the partners to find it easy to be comfortable with each other is that their personalities are very much alike. While this allows compatibility, it does not provide the degree of tension needed for personal maturation.

When one chooses a mate considerably younger than oneself, the decision is based, for the most part, on the need to dominate or assume the role of father, mother, or older sister or brother. Conversely, the younger is seeking a strong father, mother, or older brother or sister image. At first, the younger partner is prepared to be dominated. The difficulties begin when the projections lose their force and the younger partner's process of maturing intensifies.

In later years mates of widely varying ages find themselves separated by the climacteric of the older partner. Tension is created as the husband and wife discover they are living in two different worlds. The loss of intimate personal relationship can only be prevented by a concerted effort on the part of both people to develop and nurture common interests.

At every point in the marriage with age dissimilarities, the relationship of the partners will be burdened by the constant inclination of the older to lead and to dictate, to demand dominance.

All these difficulties relate to general human questions and are not primarily sexual, but the sexual relationship can be especially problematical. When the younger person no longer seeks security with the older mate but with a more exciting personality, or when the older person undervalues the importance of sexual fulfillment and pursues other avenues of interest, frustration on the part of both spouses is bound to result. According to experience and statistics, from a purely biological standpoint, age does not presuppose sexual limitations. When these problems occur, they are of a psychological nature and are derived from widespread mistaken social expectations. In addition, married couples with a great age difference often have feelings of inferiority brought on by social and cultural expectations. For example, at a dance a young man may ask the older husband, "May I have this dance with your daughter?" Or a woman may be paid the intended compliment, "Can it be that you have a son this age?"

The much older wife may also live in fear of losing the younger husband, and the much older husband may doubt the faithfulness of his younger wife. Jealousy frequently accompanies this particular structurally sick marriage.

A marriage of two people of widely differing ages is subject to a multitude of illnesses. In reality such marriages possess the potential for developing into successful relationships, but their structures do not conform to the statistical norm, and with regard to statistics, they are significantly more susceptible to developmental deficiencies. In their case, "an ounce of prevention is worth a pound of cure." Early treatment is indispensable if their total destruction is to be prevented.

The following cases were successfully treated, but they are in the minority. Unfortunately, many couples with similar difficulties came for counseling when it was too late.

Corinne, thirty-five years old, has been married for ten years to Jim, a fifty-eight-year-old man. They have two children. Corinne declares she cannot stand the marriage any longer. "I met Jim at a party and immediately fell in love with him. Gradually he began to return my love. He has an artistic nature, and in those days I admired his intellect and wit. After a few weeks I pressed for marriage, and even after the wedding I felt as if I were in seventh heaven. Gradually, however, I got used to him, and his brilliant qualities lost their charm. In the mirror of everyday life, I began to see that Jim was ordinary, and I felt tricked by fate. I inwardly withdrew, and Jim seemed basically satisfied that he no longer had to shine for me. Sexual relations became less frequent and were no longer the high point of my day as they had been at the beginning. I merely did my duty in satisfying Jim's sexual drives. I thought children would give me inner freedom, but when they arrived, I still felt imprisoned. I cannot bear this marriage any longer."

At night Corinne had nightmares which were somehow related to sexual desires. During the day she often struggled against adulterous temptations with younger partners.

Jim made a good-natured impression. It was obvious that he had little aptitude for marriage and family, but he was willing to do anything to satisfy his wife. Although he had had various affairs, he had never seriously loved any woman but Corinne.

There were some eccentrics in Jim's family and some schizophrenics in Corinne's. Her father died when she was two years old, and her mother remained widowed. Corinne always yearned for her deceased father whom she naturally could not remember. In her youth she could scarcely bear the thought that her girlfriends had fathers while she did not. She often dreamed of her father, and during the day she spoke with him in her thoughts.

Corinne obviously was under the influence of the paternal archetype. Her love at first sight was really meant for the father image she had transferred to Jim. It is completely understandable that she gradually became disenchanted and felt deceived.

The counseling process clarified all these relationships, and Corinne was able to achieve an objective view. She felt relieved when she saw she was not "to blame" for her disappointments in love. She began to rethink her marriage and to seek a new motivation for it. She learned to respect Jim as a person and to esteem him as a good father for the children. She began to invest her excess energies in public-spirited undertakings and accepted the inner emptiness as an unavoidable fact.

Lorna, fifty-three years old, has been married for three years to a twenty-eight-year-old man, Martin, and was childless. At first they had a good marriage although they seemed rather isolated. Lorna had given up her earlier acquaintances and could not find new friends. Both partners work. To Lorna the day seems very long because she has little contact with her colleagues at work. Martin does better because he has many contacts at his job. Lorna is often upset when Martin comes home and frequently reproaches him when he is late. At first he explained the reasons for his tardiness, but soon he felt ridiculous defending himself and began to accuse her of jealousy. One evening he did not come home at all but spent the night with a colleague. The next morning there was a scene that lasted most of the day. This seemed reason enough for Martin to stay away for good. Finally the couple decided to consult a marriage counselor.

Both of these people came from unfavorable family circumstances. For years Lorna felt herself incapable of having friendships with men. "What I had seen and experienced with my parents was enough for me forever, and I never wanted to get married." Martin was the only son of a widow who had lost her husband when her son was eight years old. His mother was skillful at alienating him from the girl-friends he brought home, and thus he soon gave up hope of marrying. His later wife, however, lived in his neighborhood, was friends with his mother, and was like a good aunt to him. He came to regard her as a second mother. One day when he visited at her home, they had sexual relations which subsequently were repeated. Martin felt so attracted to this sexual partner that he pressed for marriage. His mother looked favorably on the relationship.

The prognosis of this marriage continues to remain uncertain, but counseling introduced some innovations. Lorna and Martin decided to undertake community projects together, to take in temporary foster children, and to become active in their church. In this way the young husband's tendency to flight could be controlled and the maternal instincts of his wife redirected.

Recent trends are endangering the traditional monogamous marriage. Some couples claim their marital relationship is intensified and solidified when each mate has extramarital affairs. Others practice wife-swapping. Still others believe that communal marriages, with or without wife-swapping, prevent boredom. Marriage without the ceremony has—again—become fashionable.

My purpose here is not to evaluate these experiments which exist on the edges of tradition. For one thing, I have had little contact with people who express themselves positively toward these ideas and practices. Statistics which purport to give information about these relationships are questionable and are difficult to control.

But the question arises whether a marriage should not already be considered structurally ill if it—on the basis of theoretical considerations—attempts extramarital and group sexual experiments. From my experience, solid, healthy monogamous marriages simply do not consider such experiments. It is, however, true that failures in a new marriage experience can express themselves in symptoms which are identical to symptoms of the sick marriage.

9: The Neurotic Marriage

Some experts assess practically every troubled marriage to be neurotic. It seems to me that this is not only a very simplistic and one-sided treatment, but also an incorrect application of the term *neurosis*. Of course, it can occasionally be said that "no person is really healthy," but a doctor can generally distinguish clearly between healthy and sick people. For example, a convalescent is released to go to work after an operation because he has become healthy. The operation was necessary because he was ill and could not work. If we were really to follow the philosophical rule "no one is completely healthy," then either all people would have to be exempt from work or none at all. Just as this conclusion would be absurd in the medical sphere, the current use of the term *neurosis* is absurd.

In the first place, the term *neurosis* describes an illness, and in the second place, one which seriously impairs a person's capacity to enjoy life, makes the practice of a profession difficult or impossible, and blocks relationships with fellow human beings. Whether the origin of the neurosis is clarified by Freudian, Adlerian, or Jungian doctrine is a therapeutical question, that is, it depends upon which hypothesis works best. If, however, one considers all problem marriages neurotic, one risks placing false burdens on people, and they have all the more difficulty in becoming free of these burdens the more one-sidedly they are presented.

Mrs. Miller's case shows how a sick marriage can occur when it concerns a neurotic wife who, however, is mature and has a non-neurotic but immature (infantile-juvenile) husband. In general marriage counseling practice, approximately 20 percent of decidedly neurotic marriages evince the characteristics of structural disturbances. They offer, of course, just as variegated a picture as the neuroses of individuals, each of which can be extraordinarily different from the others. For example, a so-called heart neurosis looks quite different from a compulsion neurosis, and a character neurosis is to be evaluated differently than is a stomach neurosis. Additionally, in spite of the neurosis type, the same causes and mechanisms of origin can be assumed; conversely different causes can produce the same forms of neurosis.

In order to illustrate to some degree the multiplicity of marital neuroses or neurotic marriages, I shall present a couple of cases.

Carol was an immature, hysterical wife who married an unstable psychopath resembling her father. From time to time there were quarrels in which the husband Eugene gave commands and demanded absolute obedience. When there was a difference of opinion, he accused her of insolence and treated her like a small, unmannerly child. Whereupon she reacted like one by swearing at him obscenely and falling into a fit of rage. Once he slapped her, and she ran to her father who sent her to a lawyer. Divorce action was begun, but as soon as things became serious, the "strong husband" begged for forgiveness which the infantile wife graciously granted.

The court action was withdrawn, there were some months of peace, and then the same melodrama began all over again. During seven years this scene was repeated about fifteen times. Finally Eugene not only wanted to be strong but also recklessly wild. He went too far, and Carol went through with the divorce action. Subsequently, she began a maturation process which expressed itself in various ways. For example, she got a job, whereas before she had refused to be anything other than a housewife. Eugene, on the other hand, remained at the same job for the first time. Previously he had changed jobs frequently. Unfortunately, the children had all kinds of problems. They had also participated in the game the parents played. Whenever there was a bad scene between the parents, the boy stood up for his father while the two girls—called "womenfolk" by the father—clung to the mother.

Carol's father was a respected citizen who, however, drank excessively and had little understanding for his wife and children. Eugene was the child of divorced parents. His father, who had characteristics similar to Eugene himself, left the family when Eugene was still a young boy. Eugene's premarital friendships were like those of Carol before she met her future husband: quite superficial. The two were drawn together by love, and one could ask, What in the world did nature have in mind in such a case? Was this a mistake? Did nature pair a "little girl" with a "strong, fatherly man" and thereby overlook the fact that although it might seem "a good match" the end effect was a sick relationship?

If we evaluate the effectiveness of marriage counseling by its success in preventing a divorce and prolonging a marriage, then in this case my work was successful. I felt frustrated, however, when I saw that the couple was making no real progress. Carol allowed me to support her morally like a good father, and Eugene accepted only as much help from me as suited his intentions. When I—like his wife—disagreed with him, he swore obscenely at me. If Carol had really wanted a divorce, I would not have stood in her way, but she obviously loved her husband and did not want to make a final break with him—until the time was finally ripe.

The preconditions for creative marriage counseling work—whether psychotherapeutic or pastoral—were lacking here. The couple refused to give their attention and their will to the work of maturing. It was not that they lacked intelligence. The pleasure of gain—to quote Freud—which the couple achieved by their pathological role-playing was so great that a change in the entire situation was not wanted. At best, each expected the other to change.

My experience with this couple occurred several years ago, but it reminds me that marriage is often a tragedy, a drama with tragic developments and a tragic end.

In the following case my efforts met with more success. Heidi and Tom, a couple in their middle years, had been happy during the first twelve years of their marriage. Their family life was pleasant, and each enjoyed employment in the same welfare office. Then, however, they began to quarrel, each making similar reproaches against the other. First he was jealous, then she. Now she accused him of tyranny, now he accused her. Now he complained about her sexual coldness, now she accused him of emotional brutality, and so on. After they had waited more than a year for the difficulties to go away by themselves, they decided to go into marriage therapy. The sessions consisted of Heidi and Tom each relating and interpreting their dreams in the other's presence. I then asked for the associations of the listener and afterward amplified the interpretations myself. In this way Heidi and Tom learned to know each other on a deeper level than was possible in conscious life. Dialogue exercises were added whenever acute conflicts had to be solved.

The marriage calmed down under treatment after a few months, but the entire treatment lasted more than four years.

Tom came from a very pious family in the patriarchal mold. He felt constantly overburdened and suffered from feelings of inferiority and insufficiency. Heidi came from modest circumstances and achieved a socially higher level by her own efforts. She had a neurotic tendency to achievement compulsion which was a constant burden to Tom. He wanted to break out of his neurotic prison and longed for a wife who was motherly, soft, and dependent with whom he could feel secure. At first, their mutual expectations were fulfilled to some degree, but when they felt overburdened, the marriage collapsed. Of course, there were many adulterous temptations on both sides, but they were able to resist the temptations and chose treatment instead.

Aside from its behavioral aspects, the therapy had essentially three factors: (1) for a long time the couple interpreted their dreams according to the Oedipus or Electra theme; (2) we gradually arrived at elucidations characteristic of the individuation theory of Carl Jung; (3) the couple practiced the art of dialogue and mastered it.

The result of this therapy was not only a stabilization and consolidation of the marriage but also its maturation and the personal maturation of the couple. Each began to be more successful professionally and parentally. Without therapy this sick marriage would have gradually collapsed.

In the case of Roger and Beverly a divorce occurred because the husband could not be convinced under any circumstances to enter marriage therapy even though his wife agreed to treatment. In her youth Beverly had epileptic attacks, but with the onset of puberty they disappeared. She developed a decided need for dependency, and when she met Roger, she literally clung to him. At first everything went well because Roger was flattered that Beverly was dependent upon him, but gradually he developed a violent resistance to her clinging behavior. The more he rejected her, the stronger she leaned on him, and the more she tried, the stronger became his repugnance and resistance. Roger considered her a great encumbrance which threatened his inner freedom. In addition he was not given to expressions of tenderness, and Beverly thirsted for them. In this neurotic marriage, characterized by the strong polarity of hot/cold and dependency/freedom, a mutual development would have been possible if therapy had been able to effect the reduction of the one-sided functions in the partners and a mutual accommodation. But this never came about, and the marriage was dissolved— childless—after two years. I know nothing more of the fate of this couple because they moved away. Beverly, however, allowed herself to be counseled in proper behavior in any future relationship, hoping that individual psychotherapy could remove her neurotic dependency.

The marriage of Ruth and Dennis was characterized by the wife's coldness. She was a small, attractive person of great ambitions which were contradicted by her talents and abilities. She came from modest circumstances of which she was ashamed and married a simple laborer whom she from time to time despised because he was not the president of a bank. Ruth had been very strictly raised at home. When her father died—she was eight at the time—her older brother assumed the role of family disciplinarian and was even stricter than her father had been. Her personality had been constantly suppressed. It is understandable that Ruth developed compensation needs tending toward overvaluation. However, because these needs were unrealistic, she had neurotic symptoms which came over her like attacks.

If she were writing in a language class or in the office where she worked, the presence of a superior caused a total mental block which prevented her from forming the letters. The same thing happened when she first met people she assumed were her social or intellectual superiors. She sometimes fell into a type of stupor (blockage) which prevented her from keeping appointments. Understandably she felt quite panic-stricken when such breakdowns occurred.

Dennis was an infantile personality who tried good naturedly to accommodate Ruth's supposed moods. When one day she declared that only a better apartment could free her of her misery, he went to great lengths to fulfill her wish. The first couple of weeks in the new apartment she was indeed much better, but then she again fell into a black mood and was dissatisfied with herself, her husband, her children, and her fate. Although at such times she rejected Dennis's sexual advances, in a good mood she was quite approachable.

This immature marriage of a neurotic woman and a man with underdeveloped emotions and character also disturbed the children. At school, difficulties alternated with outstanding achievements; at home, obedience alternated with obstinacy toward the father or mother.

Psychotherapy achieved only a few changes in Ruth's inhibitions, in her problems with writing, and in her inferiority feelings, but she developed a greater measure of self-criticism and self-discipline. In this way the marital storm was weathered, and the harmony of family life somewhat improved. It might require several years of treatment before the old patterns of feeling and behavior change, but the prognosis for this marriage is not bad. Dennis's process of maturing cannot be essentially accelerated, but it is nevertheless evident that he has learned to stand up to his wife and not so readily let his sexual wishes take second place whenever it suits her. Obviously a certain masculinity is becoming evident in him because occasionally Ruth now says she must give Dennis respect and recognition for his loyalty and dependability.

In the case of Bob and Karen, the husband suffers from inferiority and insufficiency feelings which make him unhappy. He is nevertheless a very successful engineer, and his achievements are accordingly recognized by his employer with salary increases. Scarcely, however, is Bob on the way home than he is overcome by a feeling of faintness. After a few psychotherapeutic sessions, he realizes that he is the victim of a domineering father who enervated all his children but especially his oldest son. This motif is well known from mythology: Sons want to dethrone their fathers, and fathers do not want to allow their sons to become men. Bob is, in this respect, a living example of the mythological motif. For this reason he distrusts the psychotherapist and the marriage counselor, but under the pressure of his emotional distress he remains in treatment.

Karen also had a domineering father with whom, however, she identified so much that she has a masculine quality about her, evinces developed Lesbian tendencies, and wears the pants at home. As was to be expected, Bob allowed her to lead him. It is also not surprising that he is often impotent and tends toward self-gratification. Karen does not despise him for this because coitus has never satisfied her and thus does not mean much to her. She is a calm, self-contained personality, strong and self-confident. In her shadow Bob can scarcely develop at all. After the couple became practicing Christians, a religious atmosphere began to prevail at home, the tone of which was set by Karen. The four children—especially desired by Karen—obey their mother's every word but do not take their father altogether seriously. Bob's incipient authority is blocked by the superior authority of Karen.

Both Bob and Karen hold church offices. Karen fulfills her responsibility with great skill, but Bob is a timid participant. After all, he only became involved because Karen wished it, and he feels superflous in church-related activities.

Both described the first years of their marriage as harmonious though frustrating. Karen's expectations of experiencing a strong father image in Bob were repeatedly disappointed. He, on the other hand, partly sought a reflection of his mother in Karen, but he was always disappointed because he rather saw the coldness of his father in her. Occasionally he tried to assert himself, but Karen remained the stronger. The neurotic tendencies of the couple were strengthened as Karen became increasingly strong and self-confident and Bob became weaker and more uncertain. This circular pattern of behavior was reinforced by the children who followed their mother's lead and gave the father no chance to develop his authority in raising them. The less he tried, the more uncertain and unhappy he felt.

And then something typical happened: Bob withdrew into a shell, and for months he did not speak to Karen. The children too received the cold shoulder. This disturbed Karen because she knew "the children need a father," but she did not recognize that she had helped to create the bad state of affairs.

It was a good sign that it was not Karen but Bob who took the initiative in seeking marriage counseling. As time passed he had naturally been quite displeased with the cold war.

We developed relationship therapy on an individual basis, that is, counselor-wife, counselor-husband, and also *a trois* in a type of conversational therapy. I also utilized dream interpretation. I undertook paternal functions with both partners, becoming a kindly support to Bob and, in a fatherly manner, challenging Karen. In this way she was forced to seek support from her husband, thus giving him the opportunity to develop his masculinity.

This initial phase did not proceed smoothly because at first restructuring a marital relationship disturbs all involved, including the children. Only gradually did a new equilibrium appear.

When the old relationships have been dismantled—which of course might take years yet—a comradely relationship can begin to develop between Bob and Karen and marriage therapy can be terminated. For a time yet, therapy will function as a catalyst.

Anna and Jay, a young couple, appeared after six years of an intentionally childless marriage. They were in an acute marital crisis, quarreled a great deal, and wanted a divorce. At first, I thought this couple was merely in the throws of a normal growth crisis, but after several sessions, it was apparent that this was a structurally sick marriage with an acute growth crisis.

Anna and Jay had married against the wishes of their parents who were convinced that the young people did not belong together. However, they were passionately in love and were not prepared to let anyone forbid them to marry. They were, after all, of age. Both husband and wife worked. The first two years went by without friction. Then they took a long trip to the Orient. There the first clear differences appeared; Anna reacted violently when things did not go her way.

The tensions and the arguments continued after they returned. Finally when Jay had to travel abroad for a few months to take a special technical course, both he and Anna became involved in adulterous relationships. These were given up after Jay returned. For a time the marriage was calm again, but they hesitated to have children because they felt something was wrong.

Then came a period in which Jay, with the excuse of being overworked, completely avoided sexual intercourse. He had never been particularly active in this respect; on the contrary, he was quite inactive, and Anna had never been satisfied. As months went by and the marriage still made no progress, the couple decided to undergo marriage therapy.

Both partners came from disturbed family backgrounds— apparently both their fathers were compulsive neurotics. Anna behaved like her father, and Jay compensatorily tended to be disorderly and indifferent, qualities which exasperated Anna. In addition, he had homosexual tendencies without practicing homosexuality. He masturbated frequently. Amazingly their love survived to the extent that they remained attracted to each other.

I had them relate and interpret their dreams, and then the three of us analyzed them. In the process they became aware of the reasons for their difficulties and began to work on maturation. Jay found renewed interest in sexual relations although Anna, who assented, was unable to experience orgasm. She remained inhibited. The marriage gradually began to show a more suitable character, and the acute crisis was overcome. The continued psychotherapy of each partner and the marriage therapy of both together aim at a relaxation of Anna's psychical structure and at a greater discipline for Jay. Probably this couple, who have an active social life in their free time, will decide one day to have children. The prognosis is good.

Both Anna and Jay come from very religious families but their faith was not genuine. Gradually, under the pressures of their marital difficulties, they came to a personal understanding of faith, but at this point it has not yet attained real depth.

I have already mentioned marital illnesses which occur when there is a great age difference between the partners. I must mention this particular situation again because it is a prototype of neurotic marriages. From his neurotic development the much older man projects an image upon his partner whereby he sees either a little girl, a daughter, a fragile, tender creature who must be protected, or an unpretentious woman with whom he can assert himself even without masculinity. By the same token from her neurotic development the much older woman projects upon her partner the image of a brother or son, a "patient" in need of being protected and cared for, or a good comrade from whom she need fear no demands upon her as a woman.

Such projections pale with time and cause more or less strong crises. If there is no individual and/or marriage therapy, crises can nevertheless be met. For example, a couple may decide upon an arrangement; they may also develop relationships outside the marriage or restructure their relationship on the basis of comradeship. These solutions, however, must be termed pathological "healing mechanisms." Neurosis itself really represents an attempt at self-treatment, albeit a pathological attempt. Many couples try to break out of their neurotic marriages by self-treatment, but this only compounds the pathological aspects of the relationship. They jump from the frying pan into the fire.

Good marriage therapy sometimes achieves the genuine cure of such marriages. This can happen when partners are capable of seeing in each other, not only the image they have made or have held from the beginning, but the real person, that X in the human being which constitutes his essence, independent of age, sex, and other characteristics. In this connection, the famous theologian Emil Brunner said, "To really love a partner means seeing him as God sees him." If this type of love is achieved, the marriage can give happiness even if earlier infantile wishes cannot be fulfilled.

Even a Christian marriage counselor must sometimes have the courage to allow married couples with a great disparity of age who want to get a divorce to do so. Of course, one does not actually encourage them to break up the marriage, but one must allow them this option and, if they choose it, help them experience a new freedom. Demanding too much of a couple who for years have had to bear frustrations and have become more and more neurotic simply cannot be defended from the Christian point of view. An unhappy, immature, and unfree Christian is only half a Christian. Unfortunately I must immediately modify this statement because I know many Christians in such marriages who decide upon a divorce too quickly and too easily and marry another partner while glibly justifying themselves with biblical quotations. To avoid misunderstandings I much prefer to say nothing about divorce and to limit myself only to counseling in individual cases, but even such silence could of course be misunderstood.

10: The Sick Family

Some therapists will not treat individual members of a marriage or a family but only an entire group simultaneously because they feel a group represents an organic unity and it is never a matter of only one sick member. The idea of the unity of the family is, as already mentioned, ancient as well as modern, but it would be unrealistic to say that the structure of a family can only be treated when every member is present in therapy at the same time. Practical results in the treatment of individuals, who then influence other members of the family, prove that the whole can also be reached by solving the conflicts of one member.

On the other hand, there are many advantages in treating the entire family. The following cases illustrate this thesis.

Calvin appeared for an appointment because he had difficulties in his job training program. He was seventeen years old. His progress as an apprentice had gradually decreased, but what was worse, unless his work improved, he would be rejected for permanent employment. For months he had been provoking both his superiors and his colleagues with insolent remarks. Now he felt isolated.

When he came home from work in the evening, he always began to quarrel with his twelve-year-old brother. The mother, Esther, attempted to smooth things over but without success. Michael, the

117

father, was a government official and was under great pressure at work. He was usually extremely tired when he came in. He wanted only peace and quiet. Instead Esther usually greeted him with "Calvin and Lewis are fighting again." At this point he would go into the room where the boys were fighting and slap Calvin because, he said, he was the older and stronger. Sometimes his patience allowed him to have a long talk with Calvin, but always at the end it was Lewis who was right.

The two sisters, Sarah and Grace, fifteen and eight years old, withdraw from the family hubbub, but at mealtimes they rebel against the father who always criticizes and gives directions as to how they should eat. Esther defends the children but is reprimanded by Michael. No one in this family is really happy. During the last summer vacation they had to live in two separate tents because they could not get along. Michael, Sarah, and Lewis lived in one tent; Esther, Calvin, and Grace in the other.

I invited Michael in for a discussion, and during the course of our conversation he frankly admitted that he was a poor father. From childhood he had suffered from a neurotic compulsive attitude which predisposed him to pedantry and extreme punctilio. When his family, especially Sarah, termed him a dictator, they were right. On the other hand, he felt responsible for the order and cleanliness of his household, and the children had to be constantly reminded. Unfortunately, Esther was little help because she took life too easily and was not very clean and orderly. The two girls followed her example.

I invited the entire family for a session together. During the discussion I determined two things: (1) Each member criticized the others; (2) the focal points of conflict were between the father and the mother and between the oldest son and the father. The mother and the sons got along well, but only because she required nothing of them. The daughters were well behaved, but they somehow lived outside the family, that is, they took no responsibility for family harmony.

The treatment aimed at several goals. First, I suggested common activities. These were promptly accomplished. For example, the entire family constructed a model apartment and together made drawings or toys. We practiced family dialogue in which all the members had a chance to speak and each learned to wait until the other finished speaking. It was decided as a group to stop criticizing. Now when Calvin comes home, he is greeted by his fifteen-year-old sister with whom he listens to music or talks. He makes bicycle trips or takes walks with his brother. Calvin also offered to help the eight-year-old sister with her homework. Esther involves herself more in the process of rearing the children and assumes responsibility for their being orderly and clean. When Michael comes home, he may have his peace and quiet, but from time to time he takes the responsibility for planning and organizing the leisure activities of the family. He came for private discussions to talk about his compulsions and to learn to accept them. In the sessions with the entire family this was openly discussed, and understanding for his emotional problems were awakened in the other members of the family. It was also determined that Calvin had similar compulsions which caused him to behave in a dictatorial manner at work. Michael and Calvin thus project their shadows upon each other and for this reason do not get along. Their awareness of these facts lessened the tension between them, and their relationship improved. Calvin reduced his aggressiveness at the factory and improved his performance. The entire treatment—once a week or once every two weeks—lasted about a year.

The next case went less smoothly. The individual showing the symptoms of the sick family was a seventeen-year-old daughter. Martina was a business apprentice who was disobedient at home and had difficulties in learning. She came for counseling only under pressure from her parents. I invited the entire family, but the parents wondered why they "also had to go to the psychiatrist." After all, it was only Martina who was ill and behaving eccentrically. I insisted that all of them, that is, the parents and the twelve-year-old sister Marlise, come to the meeting which revealed the following facts:

Marvin, the father, favored Martina more than his wife Kay. The mother put disciplinary pressures on her rival who became more and more rebellious. Marvin was caught between Kay and Martina. Additionally, Martina was jealous of Marlise because she was prettier, more intelligent, and more industrious. A typical family conflict would occur when Martina got dressed up. Kay would comment on her daughter's appearance as if she were dealing with a small child.

Marvin, observing the argument, would then become involved and would end up saying the mother was right. At this Martina would become impudent and call him a square, a weakling, a henpecked husband. Then the twelve-year-old would come into the room. Pointing at her, Martina would say, "Yes, you like her because she flatters you, but I don't let you put me down." Marlise would insult the older and in turn be slapped by her. Kay would pull the girls apart, seeking to prevent the usual hand-to-hand combat. Marvin would then intervene and pull the combatants apart, whereupon Martina would leave the house to meet her twenty-four-year-old boyfriend. The parents had many objections to him, but Martina stayed with him because he gave her a substitute for her parents. Thus the lines of battle were drawn up.

I brought the family together with Calvin (the apprentice) and his family, but unfortunately new polarities were formed with moral pressure on Marvin and Kay. Kay left therapy, and Martina finally moved out of the house to live with another family. At this point I lost track of the family.

In his book *The Family as Patient,* Horst Eberhard Richter, director of the Psychosomatic Clinic of the University of Giessen in Germany, gives a very good introduction to the problem area of neurosis in family psychopathology. In the appendix you will find excerpts from this book, including some illustrative case histories.

Pathological marriages can be not only a matter of neurosis but also of psychopathy and psychosis. Under the rubric of *neurosis* I would place physical, emotional, behavioral, or socially eccentric disturbances which are derived from subconscious conflicts. These originate for the most part in earliest childhood or later when very strong emotional trauma acts upon an individual.

Under the rubric of *psychopathy* I would place a style of behavior or reaction which shows a quantitative or qualitative divergence from normal types of behavior and reaction. There are, for instance, people who are weaklings of willpower or athletes of willpower. There are those who are emotionally cold and those who are sentimental. There are liars who do not know it because they are lost in their fantasies, and there are people who completely lack imagination; there are schizoids (not schizophrenics!) and athletes of the emotions, and so on.

And finally I distinguish among the psychically ill or eccentric, the pronounced psychotic schizophrenics, the manic depressives, the organically ill, the debilitated, the imbeciles, and so on. Additionally, some forms of illness do not completely fit any of these categories: certain types of alcoholism, epilepsy, criminality, and so on. Some therapists use other terms and other definitions for these same concepts. For example, the term *sociopathy* is beginning to displace the expression *psychopathy*. Other therapists completely renounce established terms and speak only of difficulties, disturbances, conflicts, and problems. It must be made perfectly clear that no one completely fits a definite category.

There is also the danger of branding the individual by putting an illness label on him. This can depersonalize the patient and alienate him from himself and his fellow man.

Of course, this is also true for marriage and family therapy. What then emerges by way of terminology is only an aid to develop a certain intellectual understanding of the form of illness. It is often not mentioned at all to the patient and in the course of treatment is frequently dropped even by the counselor when a working relationship develops between himself and the patient. We also know how disturbed the relationship between a couple or between parents and children can be when people put labels on one another.

I recall one older man, a "typical bachelor," who had an involution depression—a depression related to climacteric change—and was put in a clinic. There he was cared for by a nurse some ten years younger than himself who fell in love with him. Six weeks after he left the clinic, they were engaged, and six months later they were married. Soon thereafter disappointments developed which showed that the relationship was based upon mutual projections making a genuinely deep relationship difficult. When even the psychiatrically trained nurse began to call her husband a psychopath and depressive, he was finished. Although the couple divorced, the wife became sick and had to enter a psychiatric clinic.

I think also of a family in which a young man developed delusions and felt isolated and intimidated. He was able to pass through the crisis and recover without expert treatment at a clinic because of the care of a devoted mother and the support of a concerned father and loving brother. In other words, it is not the sick family in itself which is the danger for the members but the way in which they relate to one another. A marriage counselor or a therapist can help if he can not only make diagnoses but also treat the total picture.

What strikes me in neurotic, psychopathic, psychotic, and other marriage and family illnesses is the intensive projection in the relationship. Of course every love relationship is based in part on projections, but there are projections which lead to only moderate disappointment and others which yield very great disappointment. Relationships in pathological marriages and families are based on strong projections.

There is another characteristic typical of pathological marriages—the difficulty of maturing. One of the legitimate needs of the individual in our culture is the opportunity for personal maturing. Psychological eccentricities, that is, psychologically disturbed relationships with others, especially in marriage and family, endanger the necessary process of maturing.

Through psychotherapeutic effort, an individual can rid himself of his exaggerated projections and become more and more mature and at the same time grow farther and farther away from his marriage or family until finally a complete alienation occurs. Thus marriage therapy or family treatment in the interests of all involved is to be preferred, while keeping the health and the need for maturity of the individual in the foreground.

Cultures with a low level of individual self-awareness and with a strong family self-identity rarely show signs of marital and family illness such as I present in this book. But the time is not far off when there will be a similarity in the developments of the psychology and also the forms of family illness in the entire world. The emancipation of nations is taking great strides. Old forms are giving way to modern ones in those countries which only a short while ago were regarded as underdeveloped. What is striking in the Africans and Asians is that in comparison to Western countries they not only have strong racial consciousness but an increasingly sharply profiled individual consciousness. The question whether the increasing collectivization of social processes—not just in the Communist countries! —will lead to the loss of freedom and dignity of the individual remains open. A harmonious relationship of individual self-awareness and group identity would be ideal—for healthy as well as for sick marriages. I showed in *Risk and Chance in Marriage* that biblical ideas refer directly to this harmony.

11: The Pathological Style of Conduct Marriage and Family

In most cases in which the disburbance in the marriage is characterized by damaging attitudes, there are deeper causes. A psychopath would try to achieve power with tyrannical behavior; a depressive partner would subject himself to the will of the other to avoid effort; two partners with strong inner tensions and neuroses would develop a battle marriage to rid themselves of their emotional pressures. In such instances it is meaningless to try to eliminate the behavior hostile to the marriage without uncovering the reasons behind it and treating them although to be sure the behavior contributes its part to the illness.

In addition, however, there are sick marriages in which behavior must be considered a basic cause. This could be the case when the husband comes from a rural area where patriarchal attitudes prevail and the wife comes from the city where husband and wife are considered equal partners. A contrast marriage of this type—granted there are no other disturbing factors—becomes pathological when the contrasts fail to adjust to each other. A similar situation may arise when a woman from an Oriental culture marries a man with Western background. Both might be excellent marriage partners in their own cultures, but in this combination they may discover that their two worlds are incompatible. Each has a different expectation of the mate in regard to the style of conduct for the marriage. He may expect a partnership, and she a hierarchical family structure. If adjustment does not occur within a reasonable length of time, the form of illness develops its peculiar character.

In other words, when disturbing marital behavior is visible, one must determine whether the disturbance goes back primarily to behavior or to other causes which secondarily lead to behavioral difficulties. Naturally it is also possible that behavior disorders as well as more deeply rooted causes could lead to a sick marriage. It may be impossible to draw a precise boundary line, and both aspects of the problem may need to be dealt with simultaneously to effect the cure.

I remember a young couple who had a veritable chaos of problems. Annely was a teacher from a small Swiss village. Makti was a technician from India. Soon after the marriage they began to quarrel violently about all sorts of trivialities. A couple of times he struck her when she disagreed with him. There were scenes because he sent not only his but also part of Annely's earnings home to support his brother's studies. His father could not afford to pay for the boy's education, and Makti, who had a good job in Switzerland, felt obligated to help his family. During the quarrels Annely had serious hysterial attacks which left Makti helpless.

In this relationship questions of style (orient-occident) were not the only difficulties; psychological factors were also at work. Annely was extremely mercurial, had been spoiled at home, and easily became hysterical when things did not go her way. Makti had been raised in a certain ascetic atmosphere and reacted stubbornly to his wife. Unfortunately, the marriage could not be healed.

Patriarchal Style of Conduct

I remember a family that began to disintegrate when the two sons reached puberty and wanted more freedom. The father, Samuel, was a respected banker and had grown up in a family-conscious tradition. He had determined the style of conduct from the beginning of the marriage. His wife, Elizabeth, was a simple person who acknowledged her husband's intellectual superiority and submitted to his orders without protest. Obviously, the couple did not place any great value on personal maturation, and the marriage proceeded completely without disturbance. Both Samuel and Elizabeth made an emotionally healthy impression. Apparently the marriage continued in a harmonious fashion after the children were born, and they too had submitted to the domination of the father without objection. But when they reached puberty and observed other models of conduct at the homes of neighbors and friends, they gradually began to rise up and threaten the stability of the family. The more independent the boys became, the more strictly Samuel reacted. The more firmly the father gave his orders, the more rebellious the boys became. Elizabeth felt divided because her mind was on her husband's side but her feelings were with her sons. The marriage went through a crisis such as would not have been thought possible. When the boys discovered a gun and planned to shoot their father, he could do nothing more than turn meekly to a young counselor "to control the headstrong boys," as he said. The sons of course knew the father laid great stress on grades at school (it is characteristic of the patriarchally conditioned man to want to raise family prestige through studies). Samuel wanted his sons to go even further than he, the bank director, but the boys began to neglect their studies and to bring home bad grades.

In this case psychotherapy was superfluous. The goal of discussion with this couple was to help them become aware of the character of the style of conduct the father had fostered and the legitimate demands of youth in our culture. Samuel was helped to understand that style of conduct must be an instrument and not an end in itself. As long as the patriarchal structure aids the family and marriage in its functions, there is nothing wrong with it besides the fact that better individual maturing must be given up in favor of family identity. As soon as the family atmosphere begins to suffer under the management of the father, this instrument must be replaced.

Samuel had no real difficulty in comprehending these ideas as they related to his family, for he had dealt with similar problems at work. At the bank he had earlier given up his desire for absolute domination because he found out that such a relational structure alienated his employees. The family was his patriarchal stronghold as long the children were small. Now he had to renounce this last preserve of domination if he did not want to risk total collapse of his family.

Samuel agreed to relinquish his extremely authoritative control if the boys would improve their grades within six weeks. When he began to allow his sons to discipline themselves, their school work did improve, and the family atmosphere noticeably improved because the boys responded positively in all areas as a result of their newfound freedom.

Unfortunately, over against this positive case stand a series of others in which an overbearing father/husband either could not or would not change. The family disintegrated with everyone involved becoming bitter and resentful. I remember one family that remained together outwardly but became entrapped in individual isolation because the wife and children no longer wanted to submit to the *Führer*. The fronts remained adamant in spite of counseling.

The Matriarchal Style of Conduct

It is often asserted that the United States has a matriarchal system. The wife determines the style of life and motivates her husband in his work, often even politically. In any case she is responsible for the care of the children, takes the main role in church life, has the foremost position in public life, and if there is a divorce, the man must pay her a sizable alimony.

Such a sociologically founded version of a matriarchal system, that is, the dominance of the wife, says nothing concerning the style of conduct in the marriage. There the relationships may be of an entirely different nature. If the wife has charge of raising the children, under certain circumstances this can mean that she exercises a position of supremacy. It can also indicate that the man prefers to concern himself with his job or with politics because he does not get along with his wife and can punish her by being away from home. In such a case there is only a pseudomatriarchy. On the other hand, a man who knows nothing about raising children may be happy to leave this task to his wife just as a boss gives the burdensome work to the employee. In such a case, the family is not a matriarchy but a lazy patriarchy.

I use the term *psychological matriarchy* to indicate a marriage and a family in which the woman is in the primary position of supremacy in personal dealings. For example, she is able to speak faster, more skillfully, and better than her husband. She may attack him in the presence of other people, feeling or knowing that he cannot defend himself without self-incrimination.

Many wives are constantly able to cause their husbands feelings of guilt or inferiority by behaving as victims of the marriage. They let it be known that they suffer from a lack of masculine understanding and carry an enormous burden of unfulfilled expectations. They frequently create scenes in which the husband can only stand by helplessly.

Other wives arrange the family's social life in such a way that they force their wills upon their husbands, or they refuse to receive a guest the husband would like to see. If the husband wants to go out, the domineering wife has a migraine; if the husband wants to stay home, the domineering wife makes him accompany her to avoid the accusation that he is already an old man.

In my practice I have known women who dominated their husbands by making purchases for which the men had to be financially responsible. If a husband threatened to stop paying the bills, the wife answered calmly, "Just do that, dear. People will enjoy seeing your poor wife in rags." Then the husband would just grit his teeth and continue to pay. In one case the husband moved out to live with a girlfriend who treated him like a "man," but the wife demanded such a great sum for his freedom that he soon crawled back, begging her not to ruin him. She enjoyed voluntarily granting him a reduction from time to time.

The dominance of the woman is often expressed in the relationship to the children. A child may appeal to the father to do something the mother has forbidden. Without thinking she is harming the child, she says, "And I say you can't. You must obey me. Your father doesn't know what is good for you." Naturally it doesn't always sound as bad as this, but in softer, more diplomatic, and more refined form such tricks occur more often than one would expect.

From medical practice I still remember many cases in which women were able to soften their husbands by using the pressure of some sort of illness. Often they would get a doctor to certify that for medical reasons they were forbidden to have sexual intercourse for a certain or indefinite length of time. Or they would send the husband to the doctor who was to say that the wife's unhealthy condition was a result of the husband's emotional or sexual neglect.

The struggle for power in which a woman sometimes proves the stronger often makes use of sex. A wife may overcome a husband through hyperactivity or through coldness. She can conquer him by demanding children from him or by refusing them to him.

In an especially remarkable case the husband had to clear all his free-time activities with his wife. Only after twenty-five years and a crisis of individuation did he succeed in gaining freedom. Unfortunately it was at the expense of his marriage.

Almost as striking was the case in which the husband did not dare buy clothes according to his own taste. If he did, his wife would declare, "I cannot look at you when you wear those atrocious things." This is the sort of woman who would refuse affection to her husband if he smoked or grew a moustache against her will. Most domineering women also use the home to function as a shrew, allowing only as much freedom of movement as suits them, without regard for the wishes of the "master" of the house. The dominance of a wife can often be deduced from the behavior of the husband. If a married man suffers from recurrent depressions the origin of which cannot be determined by a specialist, he is most likely married to a domineering woman who exerts emotional pressure on him. A husband's chronic unhappiness is usually the sign of frustrations caused by a domineering wife. In many cases the husband's flight into work, a hobby, or some friendship which is adulterous or hostile to the marriage is nothing more than an expression of his masculine helplessness in the face of a domineering wife.

Stalemate in Marriage

If both the partners have the same strength, the marriage resembles a stalemate in chess. It is unable to mature, and in time both husband and wife become tired and depressive. They often resign themselves to an unhappy situation, drift apart, or console themselves with other partners. Such marriages may also be called "battle" marriages because each partner has an underlying need to prove himself the stronger. Battle marriages are "morally" encumbering and can have disastrous effects on the children. Parents and children become subject to extreme guilt feelings.

Adler showed that the need for self-assertion can act as the mainspring for power tendencies. The marriage often represents an imaginary field on which husband and wife struggle for power with all the means we have come to know in masculine and feminine marital warfare.

The battle marriage, unlike the simple contrast marriage in which dialogue helps to achieve a playful almost sporting discussion and is rather enjoyable, is oppressive. The quarreling, the silent enmity, the constant readiness to attack, and the mood of battle signify war, not vigorous debate. In his book *Fight but Fight Right,* Bach was probably thinking of such marriages in which the struggle for power is the style of conduct although his suggestions can also be used for normal contrast marriages.

Have you ever observed Ping Pong players of identical skill? There is something fascinating about watching a game in which no one can really be the winner. There is something of this fascination also in the battle marriage with partners of identical strength. It is generally a matter of two pugnacious natures who use the marriage as a boxing ring and forget meanwhile that it is something more and different than a prize fight and that the children are also in the arena. The stalemate marriage expresses a pathological style of conduct.

Coexistence

A "boring marriage," an "empty marriage," or a "dead marriage" can be the result of two people's cowardice. They have chosen peaceful coexistence in order to avoid the tension necessary for personal and marital maturation. They sense the danger of quarrels when there is antagonism and behave in such a way as to avoid them. It is possible they feel uncomfortable without knowing why. Occasionally the cowardly flight from argument is conscious and is justified by a feeling of vulnerability or sensitivity, by the fear of a breach or loss of love, or by an upbringing which taught that strife must be avoided in all circumstances. Many marriages are ruined because of exaggerated courtesy.

A marriage in which one must to a degree go around on tiptoes is also damaging for the children. Many functions which could only be mobilized by the example of parental arguments or dialogue remain unexploited in the "graveyard quiet" of the marriage.

We naturally cannot choose those marriages which would be most favorable, but if I had to choose between a stalemate marriage and marital coexistence, I would choose the former. At least in today's world it seems the lesser of the two evils.

PART III

Toward A Healthy Marriage

12: The Optimal Style of Conduct

Before I discuss the style of conduct that is necessary in order to avoid marital illnesses, I would like to go into two questions which appear again and again in practice and which concern the style of conduct. First, how much should one gratify his natural need for self-assertion and power?

It is difficult to tell which is the more frequent evil: too little self-assertion and satisfaction of the power tendency—as in depressives and many neurotics—or too much—as with power politicians and revolutionaries. Certainly either extreme is an evil in society.

This is also true for marriage and the family. Each family member has the right to satisfy his legitimate needs for self-assertion and power. At the same time he is obligated to allow other family members the possibility of realizing themselves and achieving power. If a person is prevented from achieving self-assertion and respect, he receives emotional damage, and conversely emotional damage can lead to a loss of self-respect.

How does one go about achieving the proper balance in a marriage or in the family? Basically there are two methods: (1) Seek an objective or functional solution; or (2) make use of a personal solution related to the individual. In marriage both are possible, indeed even advisable. The following illustration from my own marriage shows the practical implications of utilizing both approaches.

In questions of raising the children my wife and I occasionally had basically different ideas. We not only had to meet the problem of raising the child, but we had to work out a solution that would satisfy our needs for self-assertion and power so that neither of us would feel unfairly treated.

We made use of the objective as well as the personal method. In the objective area we agreed to divided jurisdiction; each of us would make decisions concerning the children in the areas in which he or she was most qualified. My wife determined questions of clothing, I questions of sports, and so on. In this way each of us received a portion of self-assertion, the children experienced "democracy in action," and the problems could be solved.

There were, however, situations in which this objective principle could not be used, for example, teenage friendships; so we used the personal method. We sat together and tried to find a solution by dialogue. Often this succeeded in solving the problem and in satisfying our needs for self-assertion. Sometimes, however, the differences remained, and we could not come to a decision.

At this point, we employed the optimal style of conduct. Gradually —over many years—we discovered which of us was the stronger in the prevailing situation, that is, which was the best suited. We learned from observation and experience that decisions which left the "subordinate one" dissatisfied and resentful were wrong. In instances where the stronger was conscious of his strength, he voluntarily gave in to the weaker. The principle of service, not the principle of rule, solves contrast problems to the advantage of all involved. In this way the need for self-assertion is thoroughly satisfied.

What can be finer than to give in from a position of strength? To conquer one's self is not easy, but it is elevating when it succeeds. Naturally the ostensible "victor" is satisfied because his standpoint is accepted and his need for self-assertion is gratified. The solution is found, and the children have experienced something of the secret of the kingdom of God. Christ came not to rule but to serve; he, the strong one, to serve weak man (see John 13).

The second question concerning conduct also concerns balance. When a conflict arises between individual maturation and the marriage, which should be sacrificed? Many wives and husbands have claims to personal maturing which are often blocked by marital circumstances. According to Jung with whom I concur, this conflict is only apparent. That is, the maturation an individual attains through relationship with the partner in marriage is an optimal precondition for personal maturation (see *Risk and Chance in Marriage*), and the more an individual matures, the finer and more fruitful his marriage will be. Of course, there is one condition: The stronger in the marriage must subordinate himself to the weaker.

Is there a more convincing model for a mature man than Jesus of Nazareth? That he could be strong is proved by the story of the purification of the Temple. The general image of him, however, indicates a man who was capable of subordinating himself to others. The more mature person subordinates himself to the less mature and thereby gains even more maturity. Encouraged by this example the mate also strives for maturity. In this way the conflict between the demands of marriage and the demands of individuality is removed.

In cultures where kinship is everything and the individual is only important to the degree that he subordinates himself to the demands of the family, there exists no problem between individual identity and group identity. With us, however, it cannot be avoided, and it is astounding that the biblical perspective corresponds with the teaching of modern marriage counseling. Both recommend the principle of service for fulfilling the different and conflicting demands of marriage and family on the one hand and the individual on the other.

To illustrate the relationship between individual identity and group identity in their mutually supplementing contrast, one need think only of a child of a divorce. Because of the divorce, he first loses his group identity; he no longer belongs to Mr. and Mrs. X but to the mother or the father. Simultaneously and more and more strongly he develops inferiority feelings, that is, he loses part of his identity.

The question whether under such circumstances it is better to remain in a bad marriage for the children or to divorce for the sake of the children is falsely put; both situations are unfavorable for developing a strong identity. The alternative which should be placed over against the two unfavorable choices is: Cure the marriage, the earlier the better.

Of course, if things have gone so far that a cure is no longer pos-

sible, then the two evil alternatives must be considered. The victims
—parents and children—often require expert help to rebuild their
damaged identities.

It cannot be denied that the optimal style of conduct in a marriage—serving instead of ruling, the strong subordinating himself
to the weak—is not easily or naturally realizable. It requires effort.
Domination and the desire to win is natural and easy. If, however,
one once comprehends what can be gained in personal relationships,
much can be achieved by practice. For this, the favorable precondition is love, including so-called erotic love, the feeling which leads
adults to one another and makes them want to remain together
always.

If this natural love is not enough or if it disappears in the course
of time, another type of love yet remains as a vehicle of service. Paul
described it in the New Testament. "Love is patient and kind; love
is not jealous or boastful; it is not arrogant or rude. Love does not
insist on its own way; it is not irritable or resentful; it does not rejoice
at wrong, but rejoices in the right. Love bears all things, believes all
things, hopes all things, endures all things. Love never ends" (1 Cor.
13:4–8). This kind of love cannot be disappointed because it is without projections.

There is a double aspect to marriage and the family: the functional and the personal. Love can also be evaluated according to this
double aspect. What we experience as natural love—the love of a
married couple, love of parents, of children, the love for nature—is
part of the functional aspect; the love effected by the Holy Spirit
(see 1 Cor. 12–13) is of a personal nature.

My wife's behavior may disappoint me and endanger my functional love, but personal love allows me to hold fast to the marriage
and to serve and subordinate myself to her. The diagram on the
following page illustrates how this happens.

The large circle represents the totality of marriage and family. The
smaller circles show the various functions of marriage and the family.
The X in the middle is the mystery of marriage, the Mysterium
(Catholic: the sacrament). If I look through this with the eye of my
imagination, I see Christ, the third person in the union. Now service
and subordination will no longer be difficult for me because Christ
cannot disappoint me. It is in this sense that I understand Ephesians

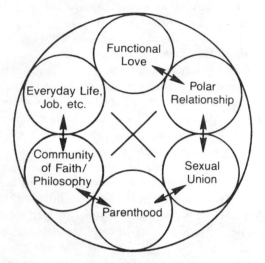

5:21: "Be subject to one another out of reverence for Christ." The exhortation of Paul—or whoever wrote the letter—to the married couples in Ephesus not only represents a simple moral obligation, but it refers people to him in whom they believe, Christ, who stands between them and actually binds them together.

And then the writer of the letter to the Ephesians describes the optimum attitude in marriage and family in more detail: "Wives, be subject to your husbands, as to the Lord" (5:22). The view through the partner to the X, to Christ, to the Lord, makes a submissive attitude possible because it does not refer to the husband in his imperfection but to an individual for whom Christ died and rose again. This occurs in faith with the help of the third eye, the eye of imagination.

Paul gives a theological explanation for this. The husband is the head of the wife; this human hierarchy symbolizes the spiritual hierarchy: Christ is the head of the church whose redeemer he is. And as if the writer of the letter lived in the time of women's liberation, the husband is addressed in like manner: "Husbands, love your wives, as Christ loved the church and gave himself up for her, that he might sanctify her, having cleansed her by the washing of water with the word, that he might present the church to himself in splendor, without spot or wrinkle or any such thing, that she might be holy and without blemish" (5:25–28).

What man could produce such a love from within himself? The view through the façades to the invisible Christ prepares the husband to experience that love effected in him by the Holy Spirit by which he can realize love, loyalty, capacity for sacrifice, service, and subordination for his wife despite all disappointments and frustrations. In this way he symbolizes Christ's work of sanctification for the church, his body, that is, Christ made the church like himself through the character of service. This love is not considered natural but as the husband's duty. "Even so husbands should love their wives as their own bodies. He who loves his wife loves himself. For no man ever hates his own flesh, but nourishes and cherishes it, as Christ does the church" (5:28–29).

And now comes a sentence which shows the parallelism between the unity of Christ and the church and that of man and wife: "For this reason a man shall leave his father and mother and be joined to his wife, and the two shall become one" (5:31).

The writer of Ephesians rose to the highest spheres when he continued to write: "This is a great mystery, and I take it to mean Christ and the church" (5:32). In this way he sought to direct our glance away from the shortcomings of our marital existence to the magnificent relationship of Christ and the church. What a marriage ethic! Then he returned to the basis of practical reality and exhorted: "However, let each one of you love his wife as himself, and let the wife see that she respects her husband" (5:33).

It is clear that this marriage ethic is not meant for everyone but is directed at those Christians who have developed a personal relationship to the invisible Christ and who consider themselves members in the body of Christ.

In my opinion the relationship between parents and children is also covered in this theological comparison. It is written: "Children, obey your parents in the Lord" (6:1). How difficult it is, however, to be obedient to parents who are unjust and who are not self-disciplined. The view of the Lord through the façades of the imperfect to the X makes obedience easier. The theological basis refers to the Old Testament: " 'Honor your father and mother' (this is the first commandment with a promise), 'that it may be well with you and that you may live long on the earth' " (6:2–3). The precondition to peace with God and with one's fellow man is obedience—another reference to the optimal style of conduct which also applies in reverse: "Fathers, do not provoke your children to anger, but bring them up in the discipline and instruction of the Lord" (6:4). This view of the Lord spares us the anger by which children are raised to be angry. The behavioral self-discipline we ourselves practice serves as a parental example. All this is not given as a moral principle but as a way to a personal relationship with our invisible Lord from whom springs the idea of moral behavior as "good."

The text here also deals with the relationship of slaves to masters, for in the ancient world slaves were part of the household. However the house or family was considered a unit with regulated rights and duties. The conflict between Christian and heathen extended even to the most intimate areas, and the biblical writer was interested in presenting the right attitude, that is, the Christian attitude of service, to call the attention of the heathen to the reality of God's kingdom in Christ.

These old texts are still of great value today because it is not only a matter of the individual's personal happiness in marriage but of the kingdom of God which is symbolized in the optimal style of conduct.

13: Marriage under the Cross—Sickness or Health?

There are problems we cannot solve by our natural abilities and talents but only by powers and actions in the spiritual realm. In Christian terms one tends to speak in such cases of the cross in marriage.

This concept is, however, not very easy to understand. Above all, the modern psychotherapist is somewhat skeptical when he hears of the cross in marriage. He immediately thinks associatively of *masochism*, that is, of pleasure in suffering. This term is often used in a psychological sense. In the actual sense it means a perversion in which sexual enjoyment is achieved by being beaten or insulted. The word comes from a German pornographer, Leopold von Sacher-Masoch. The counterpart of masochism is *sadism*, sexual enjoyment attained through tormenting or insulting the partner, named after the Marquis de Sade, a French pornographer who died in an insane asylum. Especially is there a danger in pietistic circles that under the aegis of special devotion a tendency toward masochism will be promoted which will lead not to good but to evil. Widespread flagellations in the Middle Ages under the sign of the cross indicated a religiously founded wave of masochism.

In today's hedonistic culture masochism as a religious ideal has of course become less popular, but it is still to be found in certain circles.

Indeed, not only has the church been accused of laying the foundation for and promoting masochism, but the accusation has also been made against Jungian psychology, which teaches that a life consisting only of satisfaction blocks the process of maturing. In other words, suffering is part of maturing. A. Guggenbühl, president of the Jung Institute of Zurich, explained in a lecture that marriage has a double aspect: a natural one which is essentially a matter of well-being and a salvation aspect which concerns the affirmation of suffering. The term *salvation* is here understood psychologically. It can be understood theologically or philosophically according to the individual point of view. For a Communist, salvation would be the ideal of the party; for a Buddhist, the way; for a Mohammedan, the Prophet or Allah; for a Jew, Yahweh; for a Christian, Christ.

There are some definite distinctions between affirming the cross and masochism. The masochist, usually a woman, a puzzle which greatly occupied Freud, is a priori ready "to take up the cross" whether it be poverty, incurable illness, or a difficult marriage. In contrast to masochism, affirming the cross means that suffering is employed in the service of the kingdom of God and is not a private matter. Repeatedly he or she attempts to overcome the suffering and gives up only when no fulfillment of natural needs is possible. Three times Paul asked the Lord to take the thorn from his flesh, and only then was he prepared to accept his weakness as an opportunity to demonstrate God's strength.

On the other hand, the masochist loves to awaken the sympathy and admiration of others by calling attention to his cross. The genuine cross bearer feels a certain reserve about trading on the name of the cross. The masochist understands his unsolved problems as personal fate; the cross bearer comprehends them as a mysterious act that helps Christ bear the cross in the service of redemption for the church and the world. Masochism is a part of the masochist. The cross is the tie which binds us to our partner in destiny, especially when he behaves "foolishly."

Masochism is a mental disorder, and the masochist is part of a sick marriage along with his counterpart the sadist. They form a sadomasochistic marriage in which the sadistic and masochistic behavior is divided between the partners or can be present in each of them.

Marriage under the cross makes a similar sick impression on the average observer. To one who knows, that is, to the Christian, such a marriage is not an illness but meaningful service in the great household of God's kingdom. The prophet Isaiah expressed this paradox:

For he grew up before him like a young plant,
    and like a root out of dry ground;
he had no form or comeliness that we should look at him,
    and no beauty that we should desire him.
He was despised and rejected by men;
    a man of sorrows, and acquainted with grief;
And as one from whom men hide their faces
    he was despised, and we esteemed him not.
Surely he has borne our griefs and carried our sorrows;
    yet we esteemed him stricken,
        smitten by God, and afflicted.
But he was wounded for our transgressions,
    he was bruised for our iniquities;
upon him was the chastisement that made us whole,
    and with his stripes we are healed (Isa. 53:2–5).

In my practice I have observed many masochistic marriages. I have had to treat only a few marriages under the cross, but I would like to tell you about one of them.

Dr. Hans Schmidt was a psychotherapist. His father had died when Hans was a child, and he had been raised by his mother who completely dedicated her life to the well-being of her son. She was a convinced and practicing Christian and worked actively in her church. Only once did Hans have a girlfriend; he broke off the relationship when his mother made a derogatory remark about her.

When he was twenty-eight years old, Hans met his future wife. Christina was a teacher, twenty-five years old, and also a practicing Christian. They got along very well. Christina was just as sensible as Hans's mother, with whom she got along quite well. It seemed as if this time Hans would be married. Shortly before the engagement was to be announced, however, Hans fell into a reactive depression which lasted several weeks. During this time, the relationship between the couple was broken off, and Christina also fell into a depression. She improved immediately when Hans wrote that things were now to the point that he would like to marry her.

After the marriage Christina, against all warnings, moved into Hans's house where his mother also lived. Within a few weeks the two women were at odds. The elder Mrs. Schmidt accused the daughter-in-law of wanting to force her out of the house, and Christina claimed that Mrs. Schmidt would not allow her to assume the role of housewife. Hans was caught in the middle. Christina refused any sexual involvement with her husband and became mildly depressed. The mother exhibited nervous cardiac symptoms. Motivated by a Christian outlook, Hans did not want to harm either woman; yet he was immobilized by the conflict. He developed psychosomatic complaints, was sleepless, tired, and disinclined to work.

After a seven-month triangle of agony, Hans made a bold decision. He insisted his mother move to her sister's house although she attempted to stay by having a hysterical heart attack.

With the departure of the mother, the relationships calmed, and all three felt that now everything would be all right. In reality, the young marriage was anything but healthy. Hans was a decided introvert, somewhat schizoid, and under physical or emotional pressures fled into depression. Christina came from a puritanical home and was a compulsive neurotic. She was completely lacking in sexual response and fled into social hyperactivity to cover this deficiency. The couple was able to communicate passably. They were too well brought up to quarrel, but each suffered in the other's presence.

Subsequently, Dr. and Mrs. Schmidt had three children, each of whom suffered from some psychosomatic disturbance—asthma, eczema, and so on—and two of them occasionally had difficulties at school.

Christina's hyperactivity got on Hans's nerves, and in vain he pleaded with her to slow down. She sought to maneuver him into extroversion by, for example, often inviting people over which he simply could not handle.

Outwardly the marriage functioned well, and no one but Hans, Christina, and I knew the tragedy of this marriage. Hans often suffered unspeakably from his wife's frigidity, and when she occasionally accommodated him, he ejaculated prematurely. Thus she was able with a good conscience to blame their sexual difficulties on his incapacity. Often he had to content himself with masturbation in order to escape tensions and concentrate on his work.

The family atmosphere was good although somewhat restive because of Christina's activities. Both Hans and Christina were respected in their circles. He was considered an excellent psychotherapist, she a charming, helpful neighbor and active Christian. One could see the fruits of their work everywhere.

Hans entered psychotherapy which was only moderately successful in bringing him out of the introversion. Christina was willing to take part in the discussions but refused any analytical work which might have been able to remove the sexual block. A divorce was absolutely out of the question for several reasons: (1) Their affection for each other and the marriage was beyond doubt; (2) they wanted to maintain the family atmosphere for the children; (3) as members of the church and community they felt responsible for the stability of their family and felt the importance of enduring even in difficult circumstances.

More and more frequently they questioned the deeper meaning of their fate. Why had they "accidentally" found each other, and why had they remained together in spite of grave difficulties before and after they married? What meaning could their staying in this unsatisfying situation have?

The couple stopped holding each other responsible for what they considered fate or, more precisely, a road of suffering ordained by God. They felt a solidarity in their mutual frustrations. They recognized that their difficulty could be made fruitful if they stopped feeling unhappy and sorry for themselves and began to see their tensions as a positive stimulus for service to each other, to their children, and, as individuals and as a family, to society. For the first time the word *cross* emerged in this context. At first it startled them, but gradually it became a force with which to achieve fulfillment in renunciation.

It is obvious that such an asceticism motivated by Christian principles, even though it be of pathological origin, cannot be recommended to everyone. But when it appears as the fruit of psychotherapeutic or pastoral work, it can be regarded as a thorough cure in the spiritual sense (salvation).

Like the image of the body, the house can also be used as a basis for classifying marital disturbances. In the following discussion the word *house* stands for marriage and the family, and I will distinguish among three types of illnesses that can damage the house.

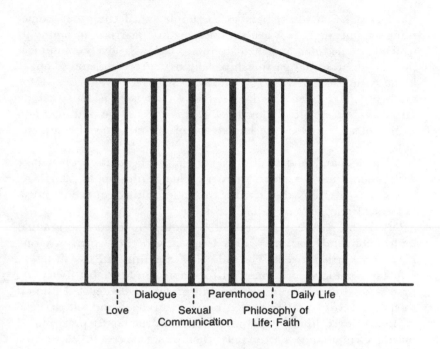

Dialogue   Parenthood   Daily Life
Love   Sexual   Philosophy of
Communication   Life; Faith

Illness of the House Due to Disregard of the Rules of Play

In my book concerning the healthy marriage, *Risk and Chance in Marriage,* I indicated that success in marriage presupposes consideration of four rules of play: (1) the totality of partnership; (2) the cultivation of its constituents or functions; (3) adjustment to the phases of marital maturing; and (4) the optimal style of conduct. Acute or chronic disturbances can be the result of neglecting one or more of these rules.

The House Is Not Complete

Have you ever moved into a house in which one thing or another was lacking? Can you remember the unpleasant feeling that "something was missing"? It is exactly the same in a marriage or family in which first one thing and then another is lacking—love, communication, children, sexual partnership, religious agreement, and so on. It is the nature of marriage and family to strive for completeness, for totality. I have often asked myself why God is so jealous that he forbids us to serve other gods. I believe his jealousy has nothing to do with egotism but with the knowledge of the meaning of completeness.

All ancient and modern attempts to replace the totality of marriage with other forms—free love, partner exchange, three-phase marriage, and so on—overlook the fact that optimum fulfillment is only possible when we strive to complete the house.

Often one partner's frustration is enough to effect the gradual destruction of a marriage. This frequently occurs when only one partner has artistic needs. The following cases illustrate this situation.

Jean, a musician, was married to a noted industrialist, Peter. At first he was interested in her art, but gradually he devoted himself solely to his own activities. Jean became estranged and felt that she no longer loved him. Several major crises in the family precipitated marriage counseling. Fortunately, therapy was successful in restructuring the relationship and curing the marriage. The disturbance had significantly damaged the child, but while she had been sickly in the unhealthy emotional atmosphere, in the new environment she thrived. Her strength and happiness symbolized the rebirth of the house.

A well-known soccer player devoted his time entirely to training and playing. At first his wife was interested in his occupation, but gradually he began to seem childish to her. She sought more mature companionship, and the marital relationship disintegrated into divorce. Unfortunately, a child was involved.

The will to completeness can prevent the sort of illnesses just described, and a sick, incomplete marriage can be cured if both parties are willing to exert the effort to achieve completeness.

Care of the House Is Neglected

Countless marital disturbances are created when individual marital functions are not cultivated.

1. An apartment or a house ought to become a home, but occasionally neither the husband nor the wife has the interest, time, or capacity to work toward this goal. Perhaps the furnishings correspond to the taste of one but not the other. The result is a tendency on the part of one or both spouses to flee the home.

On the other hand, one partner may emphasize neatness, but the other partner and the children may seem to feel more comfortable with systematic disorder. This difference can become the cause of seriously disturbed marital relationships. One might be inclined to suppose all kinds of deep psychological causes for such an illness—which indeed could be present—but in most cases it is simply a matter of style. Each person brings to a marriage certain dispositions and habits acquired from his family background. These particular problems may also be symptomatic of the contrast marriage.

2. The love which leads to marriage can disappear as quickly as it appeared. Often by our behavior we destroy the love that we have for our mates and for our families and their love for us. Without love, the home seems empty, and therefore love must be cultivated. Repeated criticism and degradation of the family members undermine love. Often love disappears when it is taken for granted and nothing is done to nurture it. Gifts, recognition of family members as people, and recognition of their functions help create a healthy family atmosphere. The optimal style of conduct encourages the development of family togetherness.

On the other hand, patriarchal or matriarchal conduct and the struggle for self-assertion may destroy love, respect, and relationships and may lead to the collapse of the home.

3. Conversation and dialogue in which listening is as important as speaking bridge polar contrasts. If real communication is disregarded, the destruction of relationships on the emotional level and then the interruption of sexual communion will follow, and the home will crumble. Having time for conversation and choosing the right moment for it are indispensable to healthy marital relationships. Partners who talk too much as well as those who are constantly silent endanger the development of a relationship on the polar level and cause the marriage to become sick. Contrast marriages can be successfully treated through the proper use of dialogue even when they have already been badly damaged.

4. Behavioral mistakes in love play, passivity during coitus, potency

difficulties of the husband, and frigidity in the wife—no matter what the origin—endanger the structure of the house and often cause the actual illness of the marriage. These problems must therefore be symptomatically or causally, as for instance through psychotherapy, treated in time.

5. Childlessness can, as already explained, cause problems, and these difficulties must be treated in time if the marriage is to survive.

The question of birth control must also be thoroughly explained both technically and psychologically so that sexual union will not be qualitatively damaged through fear and uncertainty or through unwanted pregnancy and abortion.

Essentially, raising children consists of meeting their needs by the example of the relationship between father and mother and the immediate relationship of mother and child and father and child. Deficiencies in this area endanger the stability of the home and the happiness of its inhabitants.

Children live in the force field of their parents' marriage, but the marriage also exists in the force field of the children. Children can be connecting links in the parents' marriage and a stabilizing factor, but they can also be a divisive element, depending on the parents' ability to relate the two subgroups—marriage and children.

6. The house can be damaged when the outlooks of its inhabitants are egotistical, destructive, and hostile. Divergent basic outlooks can lead to strong, threatening tensions. Differences of religion or denomination can become a barrier. When this occurs, the illness of the marriage must be approached psychologically, philosophically, or from the Christian pastoral point of view.

An example of pastoral aid in mixed marriages is given by Paul in 1 Corinthians 7:12–17: "To the rest I say, not the Lord, that if any brother has a wife who is an unbeliever, and she consents to live with him, he should not divorce her. If any woman has a husband who is an unbeliever, and he consents to live with her, she should not divorce him. For the unbelieving husband is consecrated through his wife, and the unbelieving wife is consecrated through her husband. Otherwise, your children would be unclean, but as it is they are holy. But if the unbelieving partner desires to separate, let it be so; in such a case the brother or sister is not bound. For God has called us to peace. Wife, how do you know whether you will save your husband?

Husband, how do you know whether you will save your wife? Only let every one lead the life which the Lord has assigned to him, and in which God has called him. This is my rule in all the churches."

Pastoral care can also be used in modified form with modern Christian couples. For example, a husband who has been recently converted may want to separate from his completely atheistic wife. The pastoral work of the counselor is to help him realize that his wife is "consecrated," that is, she is also under divine protection in the conjugal home. Also 1 Corinthians 13 can help bridge denominational differences which present problems of life-style.

Many psychologists are inclined to regard religious or denominational problems in marriage only as points of reference for more deeply based psychological problems. This assumption is incorrect in many cases, and psychological as well as Christian experience is needed to distinguish the one from the other and to proceed correctly.

7. Not a few marital illnesses arise through the neglect of everyday factors such as vocation, leisure time, and money.

Vocation. If a man is dissatisfied with his job, he may seek too much satisfaction in his marriage and thereby demand too much from it. The same can be true of the wife if she is employed outside the home. She has the twofold burden of vocation and housekeeping duties which may exhaust her and cause her to become sexually blocked. If in addition her husband criticizes her, she may develop a nervous attitude toward the children. The same situation can arise, however, if a woman is only a housewife. A further source of danger is the husband's lack of interest in the wife's activity—in or outside the house; a wife's lack of interest in her husband's problems on the job can present similar problems.

Free time. For the most part, the husband's job prevents the couple and the family from being together enough. The small amount of free time available requires special attention.

Money. Often poor management of funds creates marital disturbances. A common budget can usually work wonders, but sometimes even this endangers the relationship. When the optimal style of conduct is not followed, the incorrect attitude finds its expression in money problems.

Money can endanger the family when it is the central point of attention or when it is lacking. It is damaging to the marriage when the wife has her own money and uses it to cause feelings of inferiority in the husband.

Adjusting to the Maturation Phases of Marriage

As I discussed in *Risk and Chance in Marriage,* every normal, healthy marriage goes through a process in which crises of maturing cause less mature elements in the marriage and family to be replaced with more mature elements. If the couple persists in the mechanisms of the immature relationship—retaining projections, infantile styles of love, worn-out styles of relationship—false developments occur and lead to a sick marriage. If the partners altogether avoid the difficulties related to the process of maturing, pathological symptoms will appear. These may include a friendship which is either adulterous or hostile to the marriage, a too strong attachment to the children, or overemphasis on career activity to the detriment of personal relationships.

Just as an individual has specific illnesses in childhood, puberty, the middle years, the change of life, and early and late old age, so specific illnesses correspond to the age of the marriage. All of these stages can be observed in a typical marriage made under favorable circumstances between two mature partners in their twenties. Such a classification of marital disturbances has the advantage of being a dynamic mode of observation in contrast to a static one. For example, measles are essentially less dangerous in children than in older people. In the same way illnesses which normally appear in the childhood phase of marriage are more serious when they occur in a later phase. If in an early period a marriage emerges healthy from an illness typical to that phase, it can usually be assumed that things will go better in the more mature phase. There is, as after an infection, immunity.

I remember a young husband who had an extramarital affair during the first crisis of maturity. He extricated himself, and the marriage blossomed again. When in the second maturing crisis he was similarly tempted, he could resist. He was immune. On the other hand, some husbands fall again and again into the same behavioral patterns; they are prone. The dynamic style of observation permits a differentiated evaluation.

Childhood

Of course almost no illness is excluded in the first years of marriage, but the couple's relative youth, the special adaptation situation, and their greater emotionalism are fertile ground for some specific difficulties. Intense jealousy, for example, is a typical childhood marital illness. Purely from the point of view of age, one is comparatively less jealous after he has been married ten or twenty years than when he is newly married.

Exaggerated romanticism can also be a contributing factor to illness in the childhood phase of marriage. I am reminded of a young wife who one way or another lived in the clouds, completely unaware of her husband's limited financial resources. In order to meet her romantic demands, he constantly ran up debts. He was finally exhausted by trying to satisfy her wishes, and an explosion of enormous proportions ensued.

Mutual projections are common in the first years of marriage, but when they are exaggerated, the marriage is headed for trouble. For example, a husband may demand too much of his young wife because he instinctively wants her to be like his mother. Likewise, a wife may expect behavior similar to that of her father and therefore demand too much.

Communication in the first years of marriage often resembles a double monologue more than a dialogue. Such an infantile practice can be so pronounced that it causes a childhood illness of the marriage. Difficulties in communication in later years are usually different. Conversation may cease when after years of trying there is still no real communication or there is quarreling. At the beginning things seem to proceed smoothly, but each is only listening to himself talk or to whatever agrees with his ideas—until there is a great explosion.

A typical childhood illness of marriage occurs on the sexual level. The husband may persistently use his wife as the object of a type of masturbation until she becomes disgusted. The reverse can occur if her expectations are so exaggerated that he reacts with premature ejaculation. Often there are total blocks on both sides in the constant hope that things will improve by themselves. In later years when sexual blocks occur, hope for improvement is lacking and resignation ensues.

Puberty

In medicine we distinguish between a normal puberty and an abnormal one as well as between one of normal length and a prolonged one. Certain physical or emotional ailments occur more readily during puberty because of the greater tension. Among these are epilepsy, tuberculosis, and mental illness.

By the same token, a puberty illness in marriage occurs when the normal crisis of maturing appears with abnormal force and makes adjustment difficult or impossible.

The example of prolonged physical puberty can also be transferred to marriage counseling. I have known cases in which the first maturation crisis was so poorly handled that it led to chronic marital difficulties. And then I have known cases in which the unsolved problems of the first crisis continued to the second, which was made even more intense than would have otherwise been the case.

Just as epilepsy can break out for the first time in puberty, a maturation crisis can lead to a broken marriage for people who are so inclined. It can also lead to the mental collapse of one or both partners if they can no longer handle the tensions and disappointments. I remember a young husband who in the midst of a—as it seemed to me at the time—not terribly bad crisis of maturing lost courage and hope and surprisingly shot himself through the head. It was like a short circuit.

The Middle Years

The great watershed of marriage illnesses understandably occurs in the middle years. Whatever there are of difficulties or illnesses in marriage and family can be found in this phase. During this period everything is much more passionate and violent than in the other phases.

Since my wife and I have a pronounced contrast marriage, you will not be surprised to learn that we constantly have lively dialogues. But with good conscience I can attest that they were the most violent in the middle years. Now, after thirty-five years of marriage, they are less intense. Age is good for something!

The Climacteric

In the climacteric years certain marital illnesses become especially noticeable. On the one hand, they are related to the mental and physical changeover of the partners, and on the other they are characterized by special circumstances of marriage and the family. For example, the marriage polarizes itself in the middle years when there are children, but only when the marriage is in the second crisis of maturing and the children are in puberty is there an especially strong polarization. The daughter may take the father's side and supplant the mother in his favor, or the son may hold to the mother to assert himself against the father and to supplant him.

Depressions in the forties create complicated symptoms in the changing marriage which scarcely ever appear in any other phase.

As in the puberty of marriage, also in the climacteric, there is the danger of the complication, prolongation, and eruption of difficulties. It is now that a man leaves his wife to marry a young girl. Now a wife becomes depressed and isolates herself from her husband. Short circuits of all sorts occur making it difficult to determine whether the crises are normal and average or pathological. An enormous melancholy pervades countless marriages during this time of life.

Older Marriages

Older marriages often suffer from the difficulty of restructuring. If there is no adaptation, chronic symptoms occur which are characterized by emptiness. A couple who seldom quarreled may begin to have frequent arguments because new expectations cannot be fulfilled by the partner. Joint loneliness is a typical illness of these years if both partners were too attached to the children who have now left home.

We often attach a romantic image to marriages that are sixty or more years old, and there are indeed beautiful marriages of many years which to a degree resemble the autumn colors of the forest. However, many older marriages are characterized by great emotional pain. The fear of dying, personal isolation, and physical exhaustion can combine to bring an autumnal relationship anything but peace and contentment. Such marriages may also bear traces of old marital wounds that have not healed or that have healed poorly. Marriages of many years also require the help of the specialist, and just as gerontologists now deal with the special social and physical problems attendant to the aging process, increasing life expectancy will also produce counselors who specialize in treating marital illnesses of the elderly.

Illnesses of the Marriage and Family Where Psychological or Character Anomalies Are Present in the Marriage or in Family Members

In our symbolic house, the pillars represent men and women. What should they be like if the house is to be structurally well supported? There is no unequivocal answer to this question. If marriage capability could be as precisely tested as a child's readiness for school, the problem of proper choice of a partner would be easily solved. At the present time, however, no such method exists, and so the task of choosing a husband or wife is left up to individuals who may make this decision on any basis whatever. We can only be astounded that most people choose wisely.

Nevertheless, some men and women who marry have the worst imaginable adaptability and qualification for marriage and its management as well as for raising children. One must question whether these people should marry at all, and if they do, premarital counseling would be indispensable. Definite mental illnesses are indeed legal obstacles to marriage, and they can usually be recognized by most people.

In general, immature partners with strong projection mechanisms make weak pillars, as do neurotic and psychiatrically anomalous individuals. Problems can also be expected when partners have extremely different backgrounds in regard to style of conduct, for example, patriarchy versus partnership.

Illnesses of the Marriage and Family and Their Relationship to Society

One seldom sees a house that is completely isolated, but it is not at all infrequent to see individual marriages and families isolated in spite of the fact they have neighbors all around. This is not merely the result of our very mobile society; people have a peculiar tendency to isolate themselves. Unfortunately, a sort of psychological inbreeding occurs by which the members of a family lose their vitality because they are without the stimuli of the environment.

The isolated family can become overly aggressive toward one another because the feelings that might properly be directed toward neighbors or the community in general must of necessity be relieved in the family context. One often encounters extreme egotism in a family that lives to itself. When a family is not voluntarily isolated but—for example, because of racial or national discrimination—is forced into a ghetto, hostility develops. In the absence of the real perpetrators of the isolation, this hostility is sometimes vented upon the closest family members. I remember one old couple from North Germany who immigrated to a Swiss village, felt totally alone, and committed double suicide by hanging.

Conversely, a family disintegrates when it has too many social contacts. An overabundance of outside relationships can impinge on the personal relationships which thrive in intimacy. If one gets too involved in a multitude of interrelationships with neighbors and friends, often that vitality which is proper between couples and between parents and children is lost. In such a case, it would be healthy to withdraw from society for at least a time.

Finally, there are those social influences which endanger the integrity, the style, and the stability of a family—easy morals, drugs, a conformist social attitude, preoccupation with prestige, and so on.

If we compare the classification of marital disturbances symbolized by the house, we see that it does not matter what sort of image we use for marriage and the family. We can easily get an idea of what we consider healthy and what we consider sick. I use both images, but I prefer the image of the house because it reminds me of the house in which we shall live with God in eternity (Rev. 21:1) and because, as Joshua said, I and my house want to serve the Lord.

Appendix

CORRESPONDENCE BETWEEN FREUD
AND THE MOTHER OF A HOMOSEXUAL

In April 1935 a distraught American mother wrote to Sigmund Freud concerning her two sons and their homosexuality. He very promptly replied although at the time he was dying of cancer. Many years later this same mother sent Freud's answer to Dr. Kinsey with this note: "Herewith I enclose a letter from a great and good man which you may retain. From a Grateful Mother." The letter was published in the April 1951 *American Journal of Psychiatry.* Accordingly in spring of that year the mother's letter appeared in the *Frankfurter Rundschau.*

Both the problems of the mother and Freud's insights are as pertinent today as they were in 1935 and so are included here.

The mother wrote:

For a long time I have intended to take part as a woman in the discussion of Paragraph 175 which places homosexuality under punishment of law in Germany. This intention was never carried out because of my son's resistance. He said it would be of no use. I believe, however, that it is necessary to awaken public understanding of these unhappy people before the law will ever be changed. The impulse to finally write you was given by your article of January 24. Your arguments there gave me hope that these lines of mine would be published.

I have the authority to write by the unspeakable suffering I have endured all my life because of these things. In 1930 I lost a son from my first marriage. At the age of twenty-two he drowned while swimming. I know, however, from a letter left behind for me that he sought death because he was in danger of becoming involved in a court case because of Paragraph 175. I knew of his unfortunate tendency from the time he was eighteen and sought to make his difficult life easier. What cares and distress accompany this affliction can only be told by a mother who has experienced it through her son.

From my second marriage in 1928 there was only one child. I prayed it would be a girl, but fate chose otherwise. I deliberately gave the boy a strict upbringing and sought to keep him away from anything which might endanger him, but my efforts were in vain. My supposition that he too had the unfortunate tendency of his half-brother became a certainty. I have tried everything to direct my child to another path, but nature is stronger. What can a person do against his deepest predisposition? This drive is given him by nature as his fate, and he must see how he can best live with it.

I would just like to ask all those who are responsible: What would you do if your son were among the unfortunate? There are sufficient legal determinations, so far as I have been instructed, which assure the protection of the young and dependent. One must finally put blackmailers and other such evil creatures in this area out of business. It would be a salvation for me if our laws would finally be changed (in many countries this has already been done). I live now in the constant fear that my son, my one and all, whom the fates have left me, also could be driven to his death.

April 9, 1935

Dear Mrs. . . .

I gather from your letter that your son is a homosexual. I am most impressed by the fact that you do not mention this term yourself in your information about him. May I question you why you avoid it? Homosexuality is assuredly no advantage, but it is nothing to be ashamed of, no vice, no degradation, it cannot be classified as an illness; we consider it to be a variation of the sexual function, produced by a certain arrest of sexual development. Many highly respectable individuals of ancient and modern times have been homosexuals, several of the greatest men among them. (Plato, Michelangelo, Leonardo da Vinci, etc.) It is a great injustice to persecute homosexuality as a crime—and a cruelty, too. If you do not believe me, read the books of Havelock Ellis.

By asking me if I can help you mean, I suppose, if I can abolish homosexuality and make normal heterosexuality take its place. The answer is, in a general way we cannot promise to achieve it. In a certain number of cases we succeed in developing the blighted germs of heterosexual tendencies, which are present in every homosexual, in the majority of cases it is no more possible. It is a question of the quality and the age of the individual. The result of treatment cannot be predicted.

What analysis can do for your son runs in a different line. If he is unhappy, neurotic, torn by conflicts, inhibited in his social life, analysis may bring him harmony, peace of mind, full efficiency, whether he remains a homosexual or gets changed.

If you make up your mind he should have analysis with me—I don't expect you will—he had [sic] to come over to Vienna. I have no intention of leaving here. However, don't neglect to give me your answer. Sincerely yours with kind wishes

Freud

P.S.: I did not find it diffcult to read your handwriting. Hope you will not find my writing and my English a harder task.

GUIDE FOR DIVORCED PARENTS

Dear Parent:

Divorce has sealed a chapter of your life which in its last phases probably leaves a most painful memory. I do not intend to go into that, but I ask you to read this leaflet because it will help you improve the future development of your child.

Although many people can be outwardly separated by divorce, they are not separated in the hearts of their children. The miseries and deficiencies in the development of children of divorce originate in the discords which result from the inner wish of children for unity and the outer fact of parental separation.

It is up to you to help your children overcome this disharmony and to protect them from unnecessary emotional damage. Your task is not easy whether you have custody of the children or whether, in the other often more painful event, you have lost them. The conscientious fulfillment of your duty will help you avoid much of the sort of bitterness and disappointment you have already experienced, and it will repay the children for the fate they suffer.

The struggle waged against your partner toward the end of the marriage must now completely stop. If your former mate is not living up to the postdivorce agreement, do not discuss this in the presence of your child. Perhaps an intermediary third party could best handle problems of this nature when they arise. And under no circumstances should you disparage the other parent before the child.

By all means avoid a tug of war over the child. Competing for the child's favor, making the other parent seem contemptible in the child's eyes, and burdening the child with the indiscretions of the former partner can cause enormous developmental deficiencies in the child's personality. Certainly the child has the need and also the right to know why he or she must live with only one of the parents. This fact alone leads to feelings of inferiority which have special significance as the child relates to peers. Here you need to prove that you, as an adult and as a parent, can speak tenderly and tactfully about the sad events—or can even be silent. If the child feels or hears that you understand divorce as a tragic problem and the unavoidable result of general human failure and not as the immediate consequences of the evil behavior of your former partner, then you have helped the child and not harmed him or her.

If at all possible, allow the child to decide whether he or she can or wants to keep to the visitation privileges determined by law; also try to take the wishes and needs of the child into consideration when making these arrangements. In case the child has a strong desire to visit the parent without custody at some other time than that determined by law, try to oblige him or her. In case, however, observing the legally determined rule is in the best interest of the child, explain the necessity of respecting it to help the child avoid renunciation and inner struggle.

If the other parent behaves badly, maliciously, or falsely and if this damaging attitude cannot be handled by legal or voluntary cooperation, try to present his or her behavior in light of forgiveness and not contempt or hate. One cannot change the effects of evil by the use of evil. The child should learn "to return good for evil" and overcome hate with love. If at all possible, the child should be spared conflicts with a stepparent. If you have, in spite of all doubts— whether they be psychological or religious—decided upon remarriage, consider the child. Universally valid advice is not possible here; so I strongly advise you to seek the counsel of a psychologist, marriage counselor, minister, or some other individual similarly qualified and familiar with the problems of marriage and the family. If the child should become difficult and change his or her previous behavior, call in a child counselor.

And finally, do not remain alone with those personal problems and difficulties which have arisen as a result of divorce. Overcome your shyness and allow yourself to be helped. If this is financially impossible, go to a minister or family welfare worker. If there are emotional problems, consult a marriage counselor, a doctor, or a minister; and in problems of raising the child, see a pediatrician, child counselor, or child psychotherapist. In instances of conflict with your former mate, get the help of a marriage counselor, a minister, a family welfare worker, or an appropriate authority. If the child has difficulty at school, consult first with the teacher.

NEUROSIS IN FAMILY PSYCHOPATHOLOGY: SOME WORDS FROM HORST EBERHARD RICHTER

In his book *The Family As Patient,* Horst Eberhard Richter, director of the Psychosomatic Clinic of the University of Giessen in Germany, gives a good introduction to the problem of neurosis in family psychopathology. He makes a basic distinction between family symptom neuroses and family character neuroses. He writes:

The discovery of the close psychic dependency that prevails in many families complicates the problems of description and diagnosis in psychological medicine. A psychic disturbance is not exclusively the concern of the stricken individual but may have to do principally with the family as a whole. Many psychogenic disturbances can be effectively grasped only when they are seen not as individual illnesses but as marriage or family neuroses (p. 48).

Richter continues: "Psychological medicine no longer makes sense simply as individual medicine" (p. 48).

Concerning family symptom neurosis Richter writes:

In a *family symptom neurosis,* the family or sometimes a part of it makes one of its members (occasionally more than one) sick and treats him as a "case." Powerful pressure is exerted on this individual until he cannot cope, usually with accompanying medical symptoms, sometimes too with signs of demoralization. Thus the rest of the family provide themselves with a release by inducing their "victim's" breakdown. Just as a conversion hysteric can drain off part of the tension of his unresolved conflict through a localized conversion symptom, so a neurotic family can drain away part of its internal group tension by producing a manifest disturbance in a convenient member. One might then describe this member as the family's "local symptom" (p. 49).

Richter quotes B. Mittelmann to explain the meaning of this transferral of a neurosis from one member of the family to the other:

In 1944 Mittelmann described partnerships "in which the needs of one individual are satisfied and his anxiety kept at a minimum by the behavior of the other who, in turn, is satisfied only in part while many of his cravings remain unsatisfied and his anxiety is aroused. Thus one individual appears well whereas the other is manifestly sick" (p. 49).

Richter continues:

In this way, one part of the family escapes an outbreak of neurotic illness by imposing its unsolved problems upon another part. This compensatory division of roles is demonstrated by the fact that, repeatedly, the therapeutic improvement of a neurotic person may lead to the appearance of symptoms or the increased severity of symptoms in someone close to him. . . .

It is characteristic of the symptom-neurotic family that a division takes place within it. That part of the family which develops symptoms or is socially unacceptable is isolated by the others. The "victim" is more or less isolated within the family. In flagrant cases it comes to actual expulsion. . . .

In contrast to the family symptom neurosis, the *family character neurosis* occurs when the "collective ego" of the family undergoes a change under the pressure of an unresolved conflict. The family builds itself a neurotic world, often with the aid of an ideology, which in some way serves to compensate for the inner tension of the neurotic family conflict.

The distinguishing mark of a family character neurosis is that no expulsion or other discriminatory isolation of the symptom bearer occurs. In general, the family suffering from a character neurosis does not consist of two parts—one healthy, one sick—but gradually forms an ensemble of remarkable uniformity.

This ensemble is maintained, indeed sometimes even strengthened in its solidarity, if a member of the family becomes manifestly ill. The symptom bearer in a character-neurotic family is as a rule no outsider, or is not under reproach and threatened with rejection, but is rather a guiding member of the family group. The rest tend to over-identify with him. This can go to the extent of reinterpreting the family symptoms as the expression of something of great value and can be made the core of a paranoid ideology.

The real sickness of the character-neurotic family is that it creates an insane world for itself. A change occurs in its inner "nature." It establishes an egosyntonic system of values which, seen from the outside, is badly distorted. This "madness" originated and is sustained through the influence of that member of the family who is sickest. He would immediately break down if he did not succeed in falsifying the picture of reality for himself and for the rest of the family sufficiently to preserve his own inner equilibrium. . . .

Families with marked systematic character neuroses remind the outside observer of . . . those families which at the deathbed of a cancer patient stage a play full of cheerful observations, in order to spare him and themselves a confrontation with terrifying reality (pp. 49–52).

Richter believes he can distinguish three types of character neurotic families based upon specific motifs or means of expression:

. . . the anxiety-neurotic family believes in a world resembling a peaceful *sanitorium*; the paranoid family sees all its problems as though through the embrasures of its imaginary *fortress*; and the hysterical family turns the whole world, in fantasy, into a *theater*.

Now one might think that a family with this kind of limited or distorted vision of reality would have to isolate itself from society. But this assumption is not always accurate. Character-neurotic changes in the "group ego" frequently take place in outside society too. Under the influence of a collective trend, many families may orient themselves at the same time to a neurotic alteration of their concept of reality. There is much evidence, for instance, that at the present time social circumstances favor the anxiety-neurotic family type. That is to say, many families, by means of avoidance and denial tactics, cling to the illusion of a peaceful, good, well-ordered world, in order to spare themselves the terrifying confrontation with existing social conflict and injustice (pp. 52–53).

As illustration of symptom neurotic families, Richter gives three cases. These can only be outlined here. In the first case a very sensitive but ambitious and strong-willed woman art dealer was married to a substantially older professor. She managed by her subconsciously motivated behavior to put her husband in a clinic for the depressions she had caused with her domineering demands. After he was cured and released, the game began again from the beginning until the wife one day exclaimed, "I liked you better when you were depressed!" Such a case is strongly reminiscent of the typical alcoholic marriage in which the man has the problem and is admitted to a clinic for treatment. The marriage becomes calm, but scarcely does he come home when the psychological role-playing resumes. Finally the wife exclaims, "I liked you better as an alcoholic."

In a second case there is a game of alternation between impotence and frigidity. Richter tells of a man who, out of a need to over-compensate for his lack of self-confidence, married a frigid woman so that he could seem very potent. Scarcely was her frigidity cured than he gradually withdrew from her to cloak his weakness. Naturally he found some "rational" explanation for his coolness. At any rate, the game could start over again as he manipulated his uncertainty. Thus a marriage with a frigid or an impotent husband should not be treated unilaterally but bilaterally, with both partners at the same time. As Richter says:

The overt sexual disturbance of the one partner is, if you like, only the expression of the marriage neurosis. The apparently healthy partner is actually involved to the same degree in the occurrence of the illness as the symptom bearer himself (p. 59).

Richter's third example is classic. An overprotective mother "chooses" a child to show the symptoms and to become repeatedly ill, thus giving the mother opportunity to indulge her neurotic drive to mother the child. One day, however, the child becomes self-sufficient, and the mother falls into a depression. Richter entitles a motif such as this: "The Child Grows Up, the Mother Falls Ill" (p. 60).

Bibliography

Ackerman, N.W. *The Psychodynamics of Family Life*. New York: Basic Books, 1958.

Bach, George R., and Wyden, Peter. *The Intimate Enemy*. New York: Avon Books, 1970.

Bovet, T.H., *Love, Skill and Mystery*. New York: Doubleday, 1958.

Brody, S., "Simultaneous Psychotherapy of Married Couples," in Masserman, J., *Current Psychiatric Therapies*. New York: Grune, 1961.

Greene, B.L., *The Psychotherapies of Marital Disharmony*. London: Free Press, 1965.

Harnik, Bernard., *Risk and Chance in Marriage*. Waco, Texas: Word Books, 1972.

Johnsen, G., "Family Treatment in Psychiatric Hospitals," *Psychotherapy and Psychosomatics* 16 (1968):333.

Mace, D. and Vera, *Marriage East and West*. New York: Delphin Books, 1960.

Mittelmann, B., "Complementary Neurotic Reactions in Intimate Relationships," *Psychoanalytic Quarterly* 13 (1944):479.

Richter, Horst Eberhard. *The Family As Patient: The Origin, Structure, and Therapy of Marital and Family Conflict*. Translated by Lindley Denver. New York: Farrar, Strauss, and Giroux, 1974.

Satir, Virginia, *Conjoint Family Therapy*. Palo Alto, California: Science and Behavior Books, 1965.

Szondi, L., "Analysis of Marriage, An Attempt At the Theory of Choice in Love," *Acta Psychology*, Vol. 111/1. Den Hague, Martinus Nijhoff, 1937.

Tournier, Paul, *Guilt and Grace*, New York: Harper and Row, 1962.

_____ *To Understand Each Other*, Richmond Virginia: John Knox Press, 1967.